ELEPHANT TRUNK STEAKS
and Other
Adventure Stories

Dr. Larry Fogle
with Sallie Fogle

True Stories
from a Lifetime
of Worldwide Adventure

Book One

xulon PRESS

ELEPHANT TRUNK STEAKS and Other Adventure Stories
True Stories from a Lifetime of Worldwide Adventure Book One
by Dr. Larry Fogle with Sallie Fogle

Printed in the United States of America

ISBN 9781613798034

www.xulonpress.com

APPRECIATION

S allie and I express our sincere appreciation to those who have labored in love to edit and improve our writing: my mother Martha Fogle, my sister Maribeth Smith, our long-time friend and missionary colleague Elaine Schulte, and a newer friend and missionary colleague Nancy Sheppard.

FOREWORD

I love to tell stories. And in a life as adventurous as mine has been, there are lots of stories to tell! In recent years, I have been encouraged to write them down.

I have been a part of the Baptist Mid-Missions (BMM) family my entire life. God gave me the great privilege of being born to missionary parents as an MK (missionary kid). Born and raised in central Africa, I later returned to Africa as a missionary myself, along with my dear wife Sallie.

God has led us down a winding missionary trail. That trail has taken us from the Central African Republic (CAR) to Zambia, to Bibles International (the Bible Society of BMM) and finally to a conference ministry that allows us to serve national pastors and church leaders around the world. And all along this missionary trail we have experienced more than our fair share of adventure!

The stories shared here are true stories – as I remember them. Memory, however, is an elusive thing; I'm not always able to find it. About one of the stories I tell from my childhood, my mother comments wryly, "That isn't the way *I* remember it." All I can say in response is, "Well, Mom, *I'm* the one telling the story now!"

Please forgive me for talking so much about myself in these stories. It is difficult to communicate personal experiences in any other way. At the same time, I am very conscious of God's sovereign and gracious hand upon us in all these adventures and I do want God to get the glory.

Sallie has also contributed a few stories to this book. More than half of my life has been lived with her by my side. I know you will enjoy hearing about some of our adventures from her perspective. We have clearly identified for you the stories she has authored.

We hope you will enjoy the stories we have included. In these pages you will find fresh humor, raw emotion, moving drama, deep conviction and troubling trauma. You will find a lot to laugh about in these stories! But you may also shed a few tears along the way. And you will be led to think a bit about what is really important in life.

Sallie and I want you to share our excitement about the adventures we have enjoyed in our lifetime. Oh, yes, we have faced conditions that were sometimes primitive, relationships that were sometimes frustrating, results that were sometimes discouraging and experiences that were sometimes devastating. But we have never forgotten that God is always good.

Our prayer is that you will experience the same fulfillment, contentment and, yes, adventure in your life as we have known. It is true that your own adventures may take a very different shape from ours. But we believe that any life lived whole-heartedly in submission to the will of God will be an "abundant" life, filled with adventure and great satisfaction!

Larry

John 10:10
" . . . *I have come that they may have life,*
and that they may have it more abundantly."

1 John 2:17
"*And the world is passing away, and the lust of it;*
but he who does the will of God abides forever."

TABLE OF CONTENTS

A TRIBUTE TO
MY MISSIONARY PARENTS

Pioneers in the Heart of Africa

Lester and Martha Fogle were pioneer missionaries with Baptist Mid-Missions. They entered the "Dark Continent" at a time when not much was known about Africa, and when not much of what *was* known would encourage an American couple to make it their home.

Pastor William Haas had a long-standing passion for those in the interior of Africa who had no knowledge of Jesus. They had no way of knowing that Jesus loved them so much that He died for them – died for them in order that they might have eternal life! Pastor Haas also had a persistent itch that would not be satisfied until, in 1920, he himself pioneered a missionary movement into Africa. One day this Mission would span the globe with a family of more than one thousand missionaries!

Lester and Martha were not the first missionaries who joined BMM and marched courageously into the heart of Africa, but they *were* among the early pioneers. When they made their way to French Equatorial Africa in 1937, nobody could have known that they would end up serving forty years in Africa! They made their home for most of those years in the country now known as Chad. Their remaining years were spent in what is now known as the Central African Republic.

A Practical Proposal

As a teenager Lester was active at First Baptist Church of Mishawaka, Indiana, but wasn't truly converted until his late teens. He became more and more passionate about ministry, and in time chose to attend the Mishawaka Missionary Seminary, a three-year evening school hosted by his church. With a preaching team of several young men from the seminary, during the summers Lester made evangelistic trips through Indiana, Kentucky and Michigan.

Martha was a child when she trusted Jesus as her Savior. As a teenager, she became a member of Calvary Baptist Church of South Bend. Along with children's ministries in her own church, she became involved in the City Rescue Mission in South Bend. On Sunday afternoons she taught Sunday school there, and played the piano for services on Sunday evenings and several week-nights as well. Still in high school, she began attending Mishawaka Missionary Seminary at the church in the neighboring town.

It was in this evening school in the Mishawaka church that Lester and Martha met. It did not take long for the two to recognize in each other a kindred spirit, a similar commitment to serving God.

While still attending seminary, Lester became involved in helping a small group start an independent Baptist church in a nearby town. When the former pianist became unavailable, Lester asked Martha to help by playing the piano for mid-week meetings. This ministry gave them the opportunity to work together as a team.

Several of the earliest missionaries to French Equatorial Africa had been sent out by Lester's church. The mission work in Africa was a constant theme. Missionaries back in the US for furlough reported to the church, sharing their dramatic pictures and fascinating stories. They described wild animals, strange customs and fearsome challenges. They told real-life accounts of amazing conversions from idolatry and devilish practices! Their words fired the imaginations and challenged the spirits of those who heard them – Lester among them.

These same missionaries from the Mishawaka church sometimes spoke in the Sunday evening services at the Rescue Mission. As they told their stories and presented the great spiritual needs of Africa, Martha found herself responding. She was relieved that the lights were off during the pictures shown by the missionaries, for her emotional response often brought tears to her eyes.

Independently, the two young people became convinced that God was calling them to go to Africa as missionaries. When Lester discovered that Martha shared his conviction about God's leading, he considered the future in a very practical way. As I hear it, his proposal of marriage went something like this: "If we are both going to go to Africa, maybe we should just go *together!*"

"You Will Bury Her in Africa!"

Martha had always been a frail child. At the age of ten, she spent one year in a children's tuberculosis sanitarium, where she attended a special school on the grounds. Her last two months of high school were spent in an adult tuberculosis sanitarium, after a severe bout of pleurisy.

It did not take long for word to get out about Lester's plans to marry Martha and take her to live in central Africa. In those years, even the *healthy* faced the very real possibility of an early death from various African diseases. So from a human perspective, taking this sickly girl to Africa seemed unwise to some.

Lester was not put off by the poor health of his intended bride, but there were those who cautioned him about proceeding with their missionary plans.

Martha's friends strongly advised Lester to reconsider. "You can't take Martha to Africa!" they warned. "Think about what you're doing. How do you think she will endure those conditions for a term of four or five years? She will never last one term! You will bury her in Africa!"

Ray Bird, Superintendent of the City Rescue Mission, was one who demonstrated a special concern for the girl's health. Martha recalls, "Mr. Bird sent me to his own doctor for a complete medical exam, hoping the doctor would say I shouldn't go to Africa. Meanwhile Lester was praying in the basement of the Rescue Mission (where he now lived, doing janitorial work in exchange for room and board). When Mr. Bird found Lester there praying, he said, 'I give up! I know when I'm licked!' Sure enough, the doctor gave me a clean bill of health."

Lester and Martha would never counsel anyone to rashly disregard serious health problems. But they were so convinced of God's will for their lives that they proceeded toward Africa in spite of their friends' dire warnings.

No Ordinary Wedding and Honeymoon

It was no fancy event – their wedding.

On Thursday evenings during the winter, Dr. Robert T. Ketcham came from Gary, Indiana, where he was serving as pastor, to preach at the Rescue Mission to a crowd who came from all over the area. Martha played the organ for the services.

One of those Thursdays in March 1937, at the end of his message, Dr. Ketcham announced, "You are all welcome to attend a special event that will take place immediately after the service tonight. Lester Fogle and Martha McCuen are going to be married!" At the close of that service, Dr. M. E. Hawkins, pastor of the Mishawaka church, performed the simple wedding ceremony, with Dr. Ketcham praying for God's blessing on the couple.

Lester and Martha Fogle, March 1937

20

The newly-married couple took off for New York and boarded a freighter bound for the coast of Africa. Their honeymoon would be forty-eight days on that smelly oil tanker. Although not cabin-bound, Martha would be mildly seasick all the way to Africa. The pair must have wondered at times, "What have we gotten ourselves into?" But they knew God had called them.

"He Who Calls You is Faithful"

Lester had been warned that he should not take Martha to Africa. With her health, it was said, she would not last even one term.

But Martha surprised everyone. Serving faithfully beside her husband in Chad, then in CAR, Martha lasted not just one term but *seven* terms! She endured the conditions in central Africa not just four or five years, but *forty* years. And during those forty years this small, "frail" woman gave birth to seven children and raised them under primitive circumstances!

In their retirement years, Lester and Martha served first in a small church in Pompano Beach, Florida, and then in a church plant in Avon Park, Florida, helping in whatever ways they could to encourage the pastors and strengthen the churches.

Lester and Martha Fogle, July 1991

21

Lester passed away of a stroke at the age of 82. Martha – the frail one – outlived her husband, who had always been the strong, healthy one of the pair.

It is interesting to note that Martha also outlived most of the friends who had predicted for her such dire doom! At the time of this writing, Martha is now in her nineties. She is legally blind and quite deaf, but in spite of some difficulties seems to be in relatively good health for her age.

Through the years Martha's favorite verse – and the one she often quoted when sharing her testimony – was 1 Thessalonians 5:24: "He who calls you is faithful, who also will do it." God had called Lester and Martha, and in His providence He allowed them to enjoy long lives of service for Him. In spite of the medical warnings and physical impossibilities, God gave them health and strength to endure and fulfill His will.

Such Remarkable Faith and Commitment

I am honored to be able to claim Lester and Martha Fogle as my father and mother. I know all my siblings would say the same. My two sisters and four brothers would join me in saying, "We are proud of our parents!" They were wonderful parents and godly examples to us in every way.

Dad and Mom have an excellent reputation among all who have had the privilege of knowing them. It is easy to identify certain stand-out characteristics of their lives.

On a personal level, Dad and Mom were known as friendly, pleasant, generous, cooperative and dependable. They were noted for their team spirit, even tempers and hard work. Many have commented on their character and integrity.

On a spiritual level, Dad and Mom were people of unusual faith. They were serious about Bible reading and prayer, and about witnessing to those lost in their sin. Their unswerving commitment to the Lord Jesus and to His work could never be doubted.

Their commitment to doing God's will was demonstrated when, as beginning missionaries, Dad and Mom headed to Africa the first time with only $5 in committed monthly support, though some of their friends had promised they would send what they could. On the positive side, they had paid for their train tickets to New York, and they had the money to buy their boat tickets on to the coast of Africa. Beyond that, well, God would provide! Mom says they had "not the faintest doubt" about God's provision for the future.

Baptist Mid-Missions' policy at that time did not require any certain level of support before missionaries could move on to their place of ministry. "If you had the money to get to your field," Mom remembers with some wit, "why, 'God bless you and goodbye!' "

Missionaries today must also demonstrate tremendous faith to go into missions – we don't deny that. We ourselves have lived by faith for our entire missionary careers. But I am staggered when I think of the amazing faith exhibited by my parents (and others) during that pioneer era!

Their commitment to doing God's will was further tested – and proven – in 1942/1943. This young missionary couple had to leave their two young children behind in order to return to Africa.

World War II had broken out while Dad and Mom were in the US on their first furlough. Before they returned to Africa, an incident occurred at sea which was to dramatically affect their lives, along with those of *all* overseas missionaries.

In early 1942, a commercial freighter with passengers on board was torpedoed by an enemy submarine. It is interesting to note that the ship that went down was the *SS West Lashaway*, the same freighter on which Dad and Mom had sailed to Africa just five years earlier.

Among the passengers who lost their lives due to this tragedy were BMM missionaries Harvey and Vera Shaw and one of their children. Only two of their young children survived. The danger of a repeat of this tragedy led to the wartime policy that trans-oceanic ships would no longer carry any children on board.

This left our parents facing an agonizing decision, for Lois and Phil were just toddlers. Dad and Mom never thought to question God's call for their lives! They did extend their furlough into 1943 because of the war, but it did not appear that the war would end anytime soon. Would they delay their missionary service *indefinitely* because of the war? Yet the only way they could return to Africa was to leave their two young ones in the US during those war years.

When Dad and Mom finally returned to Africa in April 1943, Lois was three and a half years old and Phil was almost one and a half.

God provided a home for Lois and Phil (and many other MKs at that time) at the Westervelt Home in Batesburg, South Carolina. The folks who managed that home not only cared for Lois and Phil for the next several years; they also prepared them for our parents' return the next furlough. The two children, now five years older, were eagerly expecting the arrival of their long-absent loved ones. As I hear it Phil was quite shy when Mom entered the room, but Lois ran toward her with outstretched arms, calling out, "Mommy!"

While some choose to criticize our parents (and many other missionary parents of that era) for their decision to leave their children behind, I choose to recognize that their commitment to doing God's will led them to make sacrifices that very few of God's servants today would be willing to make. I honor them for that.

Again, our parents' commitment to doing God's will was clearly seen in their return to the Central African Republic for one last term of service before retirement. The previous term had been a difficult one, in which animosity, accusations, threats and even violence was directed against our missionaries by some pastors and their followers who had separated from BMM (some of them to avoid discipline for gross sin in their lives).

Dad had borne the brunt of their anger. In one bloody incident, without any provocation, a man hit him on the head with a stick. It was reported that one of the dissidents had congratulated the violent man by saying, "If I had known you were going to hit him, I would have come to help you *kill* him!"

After that episode, nobody would have blamed Dad and Mom if they had decided not to return to CAR.

But they were confident that God still had a work for them to do in CAR, and they were unwilling to disobey His call.

How proud we are to claim as our parents people of such solid reputation, such strong and gracious character, such remarkable faith and determination to obey God!

1

AN UNCOMMON HERITAGE

How Many Others Can Make These Claims?

I'm a genuine "African-American." Although I am an American citizen, I was born in Africa and I figure I have lived in Africa a total of twenty-five years of my life! I used to say, "I have lived in Africa more than half my life." At my present age, I can't say that any more. Oh well, it's still an unusual claim to fame for an American!

Another claim I can make is that the country in which I was born doesn't exist any more. In 1960, when I was nine years old, France recognized the right of French Equatorial Africa to be free of colonial rule. The huge country was divided into five independent nations: Chad, Central African Republic, Cameroon, Gabon and Congo (sometimes called French Congo, to distinguish it from the former Belgian Congo, a much larger country, which later became known as Zaire and is now the Democratic Republic of Congo). I was born in the portion of the African continent now known as Chad.

Further, the town in which I was born doesn't exist by that name any more. I was born in the simple government hospital 100 yards down the road from the BMM mission in the town of *Fort Archambault*. The colonialists had assigned to the town the name of one of their French generals. That move was abruptly repudiated by the African government once the nation gained its independence, and the town was assigned a new African name, *Sarh*, reflecting the identity of the Sara family of tribes dominant in that part of Chad.

One last unusual claim I can make is that I don't have a birth certificate! I am an American, having been born of American missionary parents. I didn't know I had a problem until I tried to get an American passport in my name. All of a sudden, not having a birth certificate became an issue! In 1951, my birth was registered at the "local" American embassy, in *Fort Lamy* (now *Ndjamena*). But I discovered that a fire in the ensuing years had destroyed the embassy's records! And for some reason, my parents could not find any copy of the certificate that they might have had. Now I was beginning to wonder if I had really been born! Thankfully, Mom was able to locate an outdated passport in her name, on which I was listed as her legally-recognized child. I finally procured a passport for myself on the strength of that document.

Privileged to Be an MK

I have always valued my heritage as a "missionary kid." I wear the title of MK with pride.

It is true that some MKs are resentful about their experience – because of such common things as constant moves, adjustments between cultures, identity issues, separation from friends and even separation from parents. We must be especially sensitive to those MKs who have faced more than their fair share of trauma in their lives. They deserve our respect, our understanding and our compassion.

As for me, I had a very positive experience, and I believe I am stronger because of the difficulties I had to face. It seems to me that God gave me a special place in life, a privilege that very few enjoy. And insofar as God required me to make certain sacrifices, I cheerfully made those sacrifices for His glory and for the sake of His work. I wish every MK could come to realize what a great privilege God gave us when He called us to serve Him as MKs!

The entire Fogle family at Kyabe, 1953
Left to right: Front row – Tim, Tom, Larry;
Middle row – Dad, Mom, Dale; Back row – Phil, Lois, Maribeth

2

A CHILDHOOD FULL OF ADVENTURE

A Child's Delight

Kyabe (pronounced *Kee-ah-beh*) was my earliest home. The mission "compound" was located on the outskirts of the small town. The compound included three simple missionary homes, a workshop where carpentry and mechanical work was done, storerooms and space for gardens. Out by the main road stood a simple church building and a bustling dispensary.

In earlier times, our brick home had sported a grass roof, and leopards had been spotted (excuse the pun!) wandering along the front porch under the bedroom windows. But by the time I came along, the rainy season rains drummed pleasantly on an aluminum roof, and our front porch was relatively safe.

The long dirt drive leading up to the houses was lined on both sides by overgrown mulberry bushes just loaded with plump, juicy berries in season. For some reason, our play often took us past those bushes, and we often returned to the house with purple stains around our mouths.

As a young child, fun for me often meant playing soccer with boys from the church (instead of soccer they called it *fooot-bahl*). We used as a ball whatever we could scrounge up – even if it was only a grapefruit deemed unworthy to be eaten, or a bundle of torn plastic bags shaped into a ball and held together with thin strips of rubber cut from a worn-out tire inner tube. Whatever we had to use as the *bahl*, we enjoyed playing the game. We learned to delight in the simple things that were available to us.

The five youngest Fogles at Kyabe, *1956*
Left to right: Tom, Larry, Maribeth, Tim, Dale

I Could Pretend, Couldn't I?

Another favorite form of child's play for me was walking the dirt paths through the grasslands behind the mission property, together with a young African comrade, carrying a homemade bow and arrow. I pretended to be a successful and famous hunter but, honestly, I can't remember ever killing anything with my bow. Even the rodents and small birds that could be found everywhere in the gardens seemed to be immune to my highly-perfected (and wildly-exaggerated) hunting skills!

Why did my shots *always* go wide? "The problem must be the arrow," I would insist. For a child, any fairly straight piece of the stick-like "stalk grass" so common in the African savannah served well enough as an arrow. In the first place, such an arrow was cheap and easy to find. And because it was so easy to lose an arrow like that among the stalk grass from which it was selected, it had the added advantage of being cheap and easy to *replace*.

But when I missed my target (again), the arrow became a good excuse. "That arrow was a bit crooked, don't you think? It looked like it went straight when it first left my bow, but did you see how it curved away from the target at the last minute?"

I did develop some expertise with a slingshot and later, with a BB gun and then a pellet gun. But more about that later.

This Could Not Be Normal!

As a child growing up in Africa I was surrounded by many unusual things. Most of them were easily accepted as normal. However when I considered the elderly woman who occasionally wandered onto the *Kyabe* mission station, it didn't take me long to conclude that her appearance could *not* be called normal. This surely wasn't the way God had made her.

Gou was one of the local "disk-lipped" women. With the wonder of a young child, I am sure I did my share of staring! I wondered how she made her lips that way, and why.

For a number of years up through the 1930s, tribal women in the *Kyabe* area had disfigured themselves in a way which seemed to us grotesque. Their practice of inserting large wooden disks into their lips made them the subject of endless scrutiny by anthropologists and other outsiders who were captivated by the bizarre.

In the first decades of the 1900s a couple of world-renowned circuses tapped into the world's fascination with this strange phenomenon. For a price paid to her husband, *Gou* herself had been whisked off to North America by one of those circuses to be paraded around the continent and displayed in sideshows for the enjoyment of those who came to see the spectacle. It was a shameful exploitation of human beings. Years later, after returning to Chad, *Gou* told Mom how she hated the experience – the gawking, the pointing, the laughing, the expressions of revulsion.

Of course the missionaries were as curious as anybody about how this practice had begun. The explanation was as shocking as the practice itself.

It seems that in earlier years marauders from the north had again and again swept into the south, raiding the African villages around *Kyabe* and kidnapping the women to become their slaves. The solution became obvious to the men in the south: if their women made themselves ugly enough, their enemies would not want them any more and the raiding would stop.

So these tribal women in the *Kyabe* area agreed to make themselves ugly. How they arrived at this particular means of destroying their beauty is unclear, but destroy it they did.

Piercing a small hole in both upper and lower lips, they inserted a small, smooth, wooden peg in each and let the lips heal. When the lips had adjusted to comfortably accommodate the small pegs, larger ones were inserted. Gradually, bit by painful bit, the lips were stretched to surround wooden disks of greater and greater size. The upper lip eventually held a disk of perhaps five inches in diameter, while the lower lip was stretched further around a disk the size of an eight-inch or even ten-inch dinner plate!

The woman's front teeth – at least the lower ones, but often lower *and* upper – had to be removed in order to make room for the curve of the large round wooden disks. The loss of her teeth was considered unavoidable if she were to follow the custom of her people.

I don't know whether the "disk-lips" of these Chadian women ever became known among their people as a mark of beauty. Somehow I doubt it! However, Mom believes that in time many of the women came to view their disk-lips as a fashionable badge of honor.

Common sense tells us that the results of this practice were not all positive. Imagine the following daily scenarios faced by the disk-lipped woman.

It was difficult to talk normally with the disks in place as they knocked together whenever the woman moved her mouth: "Greetings *(clack, clack)*, Madame *(clack, clack)*. I have come *(clack, clack, clack)* today *(clack, clack)* to visit you *(clack, clack, clack, clack)*."

Gou, *one of the disk-lipped women at* Kyabe, *early 1950s*

It was also inconvenient to eat and drink with the disks in place. The difficulty of chewing solid food caused many to resort to a liquid diet. The woman had to raise her head, lift the heavy lower disk with one hand to tip it up, and place the food and drink on that disk to run back into her mouth.

Further, it would have been very awkward to sleep with the disks in place. The answer, of course, was to remove the disks before going to bed. That left the grossly distended lips to hang loosely down over her chest.

One can only imagine how difficult and complicated was the life of the disk-lipped woman.

Thankfully, the disk-lip practice in Chad began to die out in the 1940s. The government took a position which strongly discouraged the custom. Besides, the kidnapping raids were not the danger they once were – whether because of the disfigurement of the women or because of greater government control. So the younger women did not continue the self-mutilation. Maybe they had also come to realize that while they were making themselves ugly to the raiders, they were also making themselves unattractive to any potential husbands!

By the time I was born in 1951 there were not many disk-lipped women left in the *Kyabe* area, and most of them were elderly. I would guess that only several of them lived through the '50s and '60s. One missionary reports having seen a disk-lipped woman in Chad as late as 1973.

Living in Chad in the '50s, I had the privilege of seeing some of these amazing women before the practice died out entirely. *Gou* was only one of them. Was their appearance unusual? Of course. I was understandably curious. Yet I came to recognize them as human beings – people who were valuable to God, to their families, and to all who would be their friends.

Until recently I never heard of disk-lips (or "lip-plates" as some call them) anywhere except in Chad. However through some basic research on the internet I discovered, to my great surprise, that this custom has been practiced in one form or another in a number of locations around the world. In most cases the custom has been discontinued. But in fact, for a variety of reasons, it is still practiced *today* in several locations!

It turns out that while from our perspective we might conclude that this custom is not normal, it's also not uncommon.

It Really Was *Hot That Day!*

Dry season at *Kyabe* brought sunny days under a cloudless, metallic blue sky. This was called "dry" season for a reason. Not a drop of rain fell for months. The lack of humidity made the heat more tolerable, yet the heat and lack of moisture took their toll.

One unbearably hot day followed another. The sun blazed relentlessly, overwhelming the land and all that struggled to live in it. The delightful shades of green which had dominated the landscape during rainy season gave way inevitably to the various tans and yellows and browns of dry season. The ground became parched. Wells dried up and villagers dug for water in the sandy riverbeds where water used to flow freely. All but the hardiest vegetation withered.

The months of dry season seemed to stretch on and on with no end in sight. Like the earth itself, the local people craved the reprieve of an early rain that would signal the onset of rainy season.

At this time of year the round thermometer hanging in the shade of our front porch often reached 100 degrees Fahrenheit. Occasionally the temperature would register 110. It had been known to climb to 120.

One of those hot days my father decided to see how high the temperature would climb if that thermometer were placed out in the full sun on the verandah in front of our house. In the direct sunlight, absorbing the heat from the cement under it, the temperature rose past 150 degrees and 13 degrees beyond!

Of course, this is an inaccurate – and unfair – way to measure temperature. But it does make for a remarkable picture, doesn't it?

What we can say with certainty is that it really *was* hot that day!

Dad at Kyabe, *with thermometer reading 163 degrees, 1954*

Stung by a Scorpion

I have at least one painful memory from *Kyabe*. I was about four years old when I was stung by a scorpion.

It was bath night for us boys.

Over an outdoor fire, water was heated in a 55-gallon drum that had been cut in half, with the bottom half now balanced on three stones. A pail was used to carry the hot water into the house, where it was mixed with cold water for the bath. Our "tub" was typically a second pail or a round, metal basin. It was never big enough for a growing boy to climb into it! The only way to take a bath like this was to stand beside the container, soap up and use a cup to splash the water over my body to rinse – we called this a "splash bath."

Well, the bath water was ready again and it was my turn. I grabbed my things and headed into the bathroom. Undressing for my bath, I realized that I had forgotten my plastic slippers in my bedroom.

I knew better than to walk barefoot in Chad. Scorpions were a constant threat. Although we didn't see one in the house every day – or even every week – they would appear when you least expected them. And you wouldn't want to meet one while you were barefoot!

We had been trained by our parents to always wear something on our feet, whether inside the house or outside. In fact we had developed the habit of shaking out our shoes in the morning before putting them on, in order to rid them of any scorpions that had taken refuge there during the night! And when we took off our shoes at the end of the day, we always wore slippers in the house in order to protect our feet – even in the shower.

So I knew it was dangerous to run into my bedroom barefoot to get my slippers.

But I had already taken off my shoes and socks, and I didn't want to have to put them back on again. *I'll just go barefoot this once, real quick . . . . It isn't far . . . . I'm sure nothing will happen.*

Holding a towel around myself, I scurried into the bedroom. A little scorpion was caught by surprise in the darkness and reacted by flipping its stinger at me. It caught me between the two little toes on my right foot.

We know the scorpion was a little one, because my wailing brought others who killed the critter. It was either a young scorpion, not full grown, or a smaller variety of scorpion.

Several years later I saw a burly, grown African man bawl like a baby after being stung by a large scorpion. Since then, I have heard varying opinions about the painfulness of scorpion stings. Some have tried to compare the sting of a small scorpion to that of a larger one, claiming that the smaller one's sting is the more painful. Others have insisted that a scorpion sting is more painful than a snake bite.

I can't confirm those opinions. All I know is that, for this four-year-old, that scorpion sting really hurt!

Since there was a missionary nurse on the *Kyabe* station with us, I was immediately carried over to her. Aunt Millie gave me a pain-killer injection at the site of the sting, right between those two little toes. To me, that seemed to hurt as much and was as traumatic as the sting itself. And it didn't even help that much! The excruciating pain finally settled into an agonizing ache that began to diminish only after about twenty-four hours.

By the way, I never did finish my bath the night the scorpion stung me.

Wind on Our Faces

The earliest memories I have of a vehicle was a forest green Chevrolet three-quarter-ton pickup. I would guess it was a model from about 1950. In later years there were other pickups, always Chevrolets.

To contain the bulky loads we carried, Dad built for each truck a wooden rack which was attached to the metal sides of the pickup's bed. Over that, he designed an arched covered-wagon-type rack to support a canvas covering that could be rolled up on all four sides to allow air to pass through, or could be rolled down to protect the people and baggage in case of rain.

Near the front of the wooden rack in the back of the truck, Dad installed a wooden bench on which we kids could sit to look forward over the cab. Sitting up there, we enjoyed the wind on our faces and an exhilarating view of what was ahead.

Our Chevrolet pickup with its "covered-wagon" rack,
on the "pit" at Ft. Archambault *for maintenance, late 1950s*

On every long trip, we had hours to occupy ourselves while sitting on that bench. One of our favorite games was simply to count the wild animals we saw along the road. There were times when we counted a herd of antelope (perhaps waterbuck, bush buck, reed buck, impala, hartebeest, or even the majestic eland) as they ran along beside the truck – sometimes outrunning us! I can remember Dad having to stop to allow a herd to cross the road in front of us. Of course, we saw numerous other species of wildlife as well as antelope.

A Surprising Catch

Even though Dad had no formal training as a builder, it seemed that he was always involved in one construction project or another. Each of the missionary men had to do his part to help with the building needs as the mission work expanded.

At the end of one rainy season, Dad took a truckload of African workmen out to work all day on a nearby plain. There they would dig out the clay soil, mix it with straw, force it into a homemade wooden mold to form bricks, and leave those bricks to bake in the sun. The sun-dried bricks would later be collected and used in a building project.

This particular plain was an excellent location for making the bricks, because there the workers found all the essentials in one place! The soil had the right clay consistency to make strong bricks. When mixed with this clay, the straw-like grasses growing on the plain would give further strength to the bricks. And there was plenty of water for making the bricks.

The water needed by the workmen came from the river which skirted the plain. The torrential rains of the past rainy season had caused this river to overflow its banks and cover much of the plain.

Now as dry season settled in, the waters were receding from the plain to return to the river, leaving a shallow pond in every depression across the plain. Eventually these ponds would evaporate under the heat of the dry season sun, but for now they provided water right where Dad's workmen needed it.

Arriving to begin their work on the plain, the African workmen became aware of some splashing in one of the shallow pools. Excitement took over as they approached the pool, for the splashing indicated life, and life in that water meant food for someone!

As the waters receded from the plain it was not unreasonable to expect that some fish would remain behind, trapped in a diminishing body of water. That is what had happened on this occasion. The only questions were how *many* fish and how *big* they were.

It would not have been unusual to find a few smaller fish in that pool. But the workmen made a surprising catch that day. To their delight they discovered a huge "Nile Perch" weighing an estimated 200 pounds! Known affectionately in Africa as the *capitaine* (the "captain"), this fish is the favorite of most who have ever eaten its flesh – including me! It doesn't have a lot of bones like some fish do, and its meat does not have a strong fishy taste.

If the African men had hung this prize from a pole carried between them on their shoulders, its tail might have dragged on the ground! What a catch!

The huge "Nile Perch" found in a pool on the plain, early 1950s

We Just Made Them Willing to Go!

From *Kyabe*, after the birth of the last of us seven children, we moved to the larger town of *Fort Archambault*. Here the mission compound was in town. This property included one brick home large enough for our family, another smaller home occupied by a single missionary lady, storerooms and garages, a large church building and plenty of yard in which to play.

The mission property was surrounded by a low fence that sufficiently marked its boundaries but didn't keep out the goats from the neighborhood. Well, the goats just gave us more targets (besides the lizards and rodents that considered the property to be their home) for our slingshots and, later, our BB guns! We didn't really hurt them. The BBs just stung them enough to make them want to return to wherever they came from. We just made them willing to go!

I learned to make my own slingshots, but it was so much easier to just buy one made by one of my friends. Theirs were always better made than mine, and I figured the ten cents it cost me to buy one was money well spent! I practiced and practiced until I could hit a lizard running up the outside wall of our house toward the peak of the roof. Did you know a lizard sheds its tail when traumatized? I could imagine its cry, "Aaaggghhh!" as it arched its back and fell backward off the wall toward the ground below.

Who Would Have **Known?**

If you think I was cruel, let me tell you about something my *brothers* did! (Or was I myself involved more deeply in this event than I would want you to know?)

With our three oldest siblings all away at school at the time, there were only four of us kids left at home. Tim and Tom, twin brothers only a year and a half older than I, and my youngest brother Dale, two years behind me, were my closest companions and playmates. As such, often they were also my partners in crime.

I don't know who started this episode, but somehow it seems we were all mixed up in it.

There is a tiny, incredibly hot, red pepper that grows well in central Africa. *Pili-pili* can be dried, ground up into powder and sprinkled lightly into your food to give it some zest. Used with moderation, it makes some African foods quite appealing. But *nobody* would pick it up and eat it raw! Just touching it to your lips will make your lips burn. A good dose in your food can make you gasp for breath.

As children, we knew the reputation of this hot red pepper, but had never experimented with it. One afternoon when we were outside playing with our full-grown German Shepherd, we got thinking how much better it would be to experiment on the dog than on ourselves. We got the bright idea of mixing some of the raw *pili-pili*, whole, into the dog's food which was cooling in the outside kitchen. Then we brought the concoction out for man's best friend to enjoy, and watched as he wolfed it down. The bowl of cooked rice with leaf greens and meat scraps was inhaled – and along with it those *pili-pili*.

Whoops! All of a sudden the dog registered the fact that there was something decidedly different about his food today. He took off running, and ran for the next half hour. He ran in desperation, as if trying to outrun the burning in his mouth. He circled the house over and over again. His tongue hung out of his mouth. His eyes bugged out. And he made the most pitiful yelping and howling noises you ever did hear.

We stood watching for the longest time, first in mischievous glee, then in guilt, then in argument about who had suggested this cruel experiment in the first place! Finally, we turned to more practical matters and assigned someone to fill the dog's water bowl for him – and keep it filled. I don't think that dog stopped drinking until the sun went down.

Who would have *known* a dog would react to those tiny red *pili-pili* like that?

The Perfect Use for Tennis Racquets

Among our family's more worthless belongings were a couple of old tennis racquets. I don't know where we had gotten them, or why we kept them. We certainly had no occasion to play tennis in that part of Africa! In any case, we younger boys knew nothing about the game.

We put our creative minds to work and, after several less successful suggestions about how best to use the tennis racquets, felt we had found the perfect use for them.

Our home at *Fort Archambault* was a brick dwelling with cement floors and an aluminum roof. It was designed in such a way that we could follow the hallways to circle all the way through the rooms of the house and back to where we started. What fun it was to chase each other around and around through the house, or to play hide and seek with so many possibilities of hiding and avoiding each other.

The problem was that these "circular" hallways also allowed the bats that occupied our house to circle through the house to their hearts' content. There was no way to corner a bat in one room in order to kill it. A bat would wing past us in the living room, then continue through the dining room and kitchen, down the hall toward the bedrooms and circle back out the connecting hall from the bedrooms to the living room – thereby making its presence known to us over and over again.

One of the goals of any missionary who had bats in his home was to kill them. For an MK, killing bats became a challenge and one of his greatest delights!

Especially in the evenings the bats came alive – squeaking and chirping, swooping and dipping as they flew through the house at their leisure. Time for our evening entertainment!

We discovered that swinging something solid at the bats as they circled past us was ineffective, with only an occasional kill to our credit. The bats' radar almost always allowed them to divert at the last second to avoid our weapons. But we came to realize that swinging a tennis racket, as wide as it was, was not as easily detected by the bats' radar because of the air that passed through the strings. It made a very effective weapon. *Whack! Got another one!*

Of course, our next challenge was to find the victim's carcass across the room wherever it had landed. *Is that it between the couch cushions? See that thing on top of the buffet? What is that hanging from the ceiling fan?* We also sometimes had a mess to clean up!

Killing bats may, in fact, have been the very reason for which Dad and Mom had taken those old tennis racquets to Africa, but we boys imagined that we had been the ones to discover this perfect way to use them!

Organ Lessons in the Heart of Africa

Organ lessons for a *six-year-old boy?* In the heart of *Africa?*

Mom was very musical. She played the piano and organ and, it seems, could manage basically anything else with a keyboard. She was determined that raising her children in the heart of Africa would not keep her from teaching music to them. They should have the opportunity to learn to play the piano like any other American kid whose parents want them to take piano lessons.

Except we didn't have a piano.

Somewhere, somehow, our parents had acquired an old-fashioned "pump" organ. It found an honored place in our house at *Fort Archambault*. That organ became very familiar to us kids.

By this time the two oldest children in the family were in the US for high school, so only the five youngest were still in Africa with our parents. Mom believed it was her motherly duty to train us in some skill more worthwhile than knocking bats out of the air with a tennis racquet. She was not going to let these years pass without teaching us some music!

It was understandable that Mom would teach organ lessons to the oldest of the five siblings still at home, Maribeth. Looking back, it is clear that Maribeth was worth the time Mom invested in her lessons, for in time she herself became an accomplished musician.

But I'm afraid Tim, Tom, Dale and I were not such good investments! At least we learned a few basics about music, and that foundation was valuable. But none of us were too enthusiastic about the organ lessons. We found the required practice to be intolerable when, instead, we could be outside playing soccer with a grapefruit or shooting lizards off the wall with our slingshots.

The pump organ itself was memorable. We would choose the sounds we wanted to produce by moving our hands across the keyboard, but the sound was powered by using our feet to pump the pedals of the organ. *Left, right, left, right.* The more energetically we pumped the foot pedals, the more air passed through the organ's bellows to produce the sound. *Left, right, left, right.* When our pumping lagged, when our pace slowed, the organ's volume would fade correspondingly. *Left, right, left, right . . . Keep going!*

Our organ was an ancient model that had seen better days. Surely, the sounds produced by that musical instrument were not all normal. As we pumped its foot pedals, the organ creaked and wheezed and groaned. These extra sounds added to the experience – but not enough to make us enjoy the organ lessons.

A Life of Its Own

Several times during my elementary school years, Dad and Mom planned special trips for the family. During our vacation months from school, these trips took us across Chad and CAR to visit our other mission stations.

Using part of our vacation time this way gave us the opportunity to do something special as a family, to see the sights in other places, and to visit other missionary families with their kids.

Traveling the dirt roads, no matter how tiring, was always a bit exciting for us kids. We sat high on our bench in the back of the pickup, looking out over the cab – wondering what wild animals we might see on this trip! Waiting for a fallen tree to be cut away from the road provided an interesting diversion along the way. Lunch from the tailgate of the truck was always welcome in the middle of the day.

On one of these vacation trips, perhaps in 1962, we visited the mission hospital at *Ippy* (pronounced *Ee-pee*) in CAR. Wearing surgical masks to preserve the sterile atmosphere, Tim, Tom and I were permitted to observe one surgery. The surgery may have been an everyday experience for the hospital staff, but it was a fairly traumatic experience for us!

While I cannot remember the details of that surgery, I do remember the blood spurting from the incision as the scalpel first cut into the patient's flesh. I remember seeing the doctor's bloody hands and wondering how the trauma he was inflicting on the unfortunate man could result in anything positive.

Even at that age I understood that surgery is sometimes necessary in order to bring healing. But watching that one surgery at *Ippy* was enough to bring me to a firm conclusion: I really had no desire to be a medical missionary!

It may have been on that same vacation trip in 1962 that we made our way to the mission station at *Ndele* (pronounced *Ndeh-leh*). I don't remember much about the station, set among the uninviting, rocky hills of northern CAR. What I remember best about *Ndele* took place along the road before we even reached our destination.

As our pickup labored along the endless, one-lane road from *Fort Crampel* to *Ndele*, the terrain became increasingly more barren. There were fewer trees, and the ones that did grow there were stunted. Great, jagged rocks and oddly-shaped boulders dominated the hillsides.

The truck rattled its way across rough, rocky stretches of road, and churned through deep patches of sand.

A flat rear tire halted our progress. With the help of an African man traveling with us as an apprentice mechanic, the lug nuts were removed, and the spare tire replaced the damaged one. Dad took responsibility for installing the lug nuts, in order to be sure they were securely in place.

Meanwhile, the African worker moved forward to check things under the hood.

Dad hand-tightened the lug nuts, used the lug wrench briefly on each one, then lowered the jack. But before he could make one more round with the lug wrench to complete the tightening of the nuts, he was interrupted.

"*Monsieur*, water is not much in the radiator."

Laying the wrench on the ground by the jack, Dad went to the front of the truck to check for himself the level of water in the radiator. Instructing the African to fill the radiator, Dad returned to the rear of the truck, gathered up the jack and lug wrench, and prepared to get back on the road again. Within minutes we were on our way.

About ten minutes later, as we moved through a long sandy stretch of the road, we began to feel a strange vibration under us which increased almost immediately to an uneven wobble. Dad was still considering what these symptoms might mean. At the same time, he was struggling to maintain some speed through the sand so we wouldn't get bogged down.

All of a sudden the left rear corner of the truck sagged and we began to plow sand. From our vantage point high on our bench in the back of the truck, looking out over the cab, the four of us boys saw a very unusual sight.

We were not even beginning to comprehend what was happening as the truck staggered to a stop. But there was no question about what we saw. Off to our left, there was a perfectly good truck tire that looked just like ours – *Oh, it is ours!* – rolling down the road beside us, then ahead of us!

The tire seemed as if it had a life of its own. As we watched, it began to wobble, rolled off the road to the left into the grass, tottered like a wounded animal, and finally fell to the ground as if it had breathed its last.

Why had the tire come off the truck? Dad had forgotten to finish tightening the lug nuts before he put away the tools. The rough and uneven road had helped the nuts to gradually work loose. They dropped off one at a time until finally there was nothing left to hold the tire in place. Released from the moving truck the tire took off down the road on its own, with its former momentum speeding it on its way.

Only five of the eight lug nuts could be found in the sand and grass. But they were enough to re-attach the tire to the truck, and we continued on our way to *Ndele.*

Dad was sure this time to firmly tighten the lug nuts! And with only five of them holding the wheel securely in place, he stopped several times during the rest of the trip to make sure they were still tight.

A T-Shaped Church Building

The church building I remember on the BMM mission property in *Fort Archambault* was huge. About 1,500 people met there each Sunday morning. Sometimes the crowds swelled to 2,000. On special occasions, it was common to find additional people seated outside on grass mats, listening through the open windows.

Great care had been exercised in the design of this huge building. The congregation faced an unusual problem. How should the building be designed in order to best accommodate the need to translate the preaching and teaching into several different languages?

Sango (pronounced *Sahng-go*) was the national "trade language" at the time, so it was therefore the primary language used in the church services. Yet several different tribal groups were heavily represented in the services. Many of those people needed to have the preaching and teaching translated into their tribal languages in order to fully understand.

There were two ways to handle the necessary multiple translations. Either everybody would be forced to endure three translations in a row, or all three translations could be done simultaneously in different parts of the church.

So the idea was born to build a T-shaped church building, with the platform in the center of the top of the T. The people of each language group could locate themselves in separate parts of the T along with their translator. To make best use of the time, each translator could translate for his people what the speaker said, while the other translators were doing the same. While there would be some distraction of noise, that distraction would be minimized by some separation.

I understand that pioneer missionary Paul Metzler drew up the plans for the original T-shaped church building in *Fort Archambault*, then laid the foundation before leaving for furlough. It was my father, still living at *Kyabe* at the time, who was asked to oversee the work of erecting the walls. He also took responsibility for hauling timbers from as far as *Fort Crampel*, some 200 kilometers away, for the superstructure of the building. When his own furlough intervened, others took over to complete the construction project by putting on the roof.

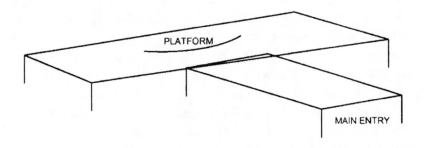

Drawing above shows the T-shape layout of the church in the next picture

The original T-shaped church at Fort Archambault, *late 1950s*

That first brick building, the one my father helped to build, deteriorated over time and was finally torn down. A new concrete block building stands on the same foundation today, and thus maintains its unique T-shape. Several times during my own missionary career, I have had the privilege of standing in that church to preach or teach.

"We Don't Need a Statue of Mary . . . . "

Dad had a reputation for friendliness. He was friendly to everyone. These friendships often opened the door for him to share with people how they could know they were forgiven for their sin and be assured of eternal life.

When we were living in *Fort Archambault* in the late-1950s, Dad developed a friendship with a young Catholic priest posted in the area. He was an American who had received his training in France. There were not many foreigners in the country of Chad at that time. The few of us that *were* there were naturally drawn together because of our common situation – all of us were away from our home countries, making the best of life in a primitive place.

This Catholic priest appreciated the friendship that Dad offered him. So from time to time, he would stop by our mission to visit. Sometimes, he stopped just to say hi. Other times, he came to seek the advice that a man like Dad, with greater experience in Africa, could give him.

Once when this priest was having supper with us, Dad called on six-year-old Dale to ask the blessing before our meal. After all, in our family rotation it was his turn to pray. The priest was *amazed* to discover that a child of Dale's age could pray as if he really knew God personally!

This was not the first time the priest had been caught by surprise when visiting our family! Several years earlier, when I was about five, his car pulled up in front of the mission house. Along with Tim and Tom, my older twin brothers, I joined Dad as he went out to meet him. The priest couldn't take the time to sit down in the house to visit, he said. So Dad stood by the car to talk with him for a few minutes.

While the two talked, the three of us boys explored the priest's car, a small Renault model called a *"Three-Horse"* (English translation). It was a cheap, boxy car that we had always called a "tin can." No luxuries here! Having exhausted all the features of the outside of the vehicle, we began to look through the windows at what we could see inside the car. We were especially intrigued by a small, molded figurine attached to the dashboard.

When he could interrupt the ongoing conversation, one of the twins asked the priest, "What is that statue thing in your car?"

Seeing what they were pointing to, the priest answered, "That's a statue of Mary, the mother of Jesus."

"Oh. What's it for?"

"Well, I keep it there to remind me to pray," explained the priest.

My brother thought about that for a minute. "Oh . . . In our family, we don't *need* a statue of Mary to remind us to pray."

An embarrassed silence followed. In defeat, the priest finally turned to Dad, murmuring, "He got me, didn't he?"

Out of the mouth of babes . . .

Unexpected Visitors

What excitement there was in *Fort Archambault* when we heard the announcement, "Prince Philip is coming to town!" Imagine – a visit from the husband of the Queen of England!

In reality, Prince Philip's jet made this scheduled stop at the local airport only for the purpose of refueling. While on the ground, he exited the plane briefly to greet the small crowd that had gathered to see him. The Fogle family was among them. We did not want to miss this occasion!

Another exciting event took place one December afternoon in the late-1950s. Our attention was drawn to a buzz of activity on the dirt road immediately in front of our mission property. There was the rough sound of a car's straining engine . . . some yelling as if there was a crisis . . . the gathering of a crowd . . . and finally shooting flames and small explosions and clouds of black smoke. Evidently, the car had overheated and caught on fire.

A Scottish family – Bob and Ruby Rickett, with son Nick (about my age) – huddled together helplessly as they watched their vehicle burn to a charred hunk of metal before their eyes. Aside from one suitcase and several small bags they had managed to salvage when they first escaped the burning car, they lost everything.

Bob Rickett had been fired from his job as warden in a prison for rebels in Kenya because he was "too kind to the prisoners." They were in the process of slowly working their way back to Scotland, when their trip was halted in such a devastating way.

The car fire happened directly in front of our house – no more than one hundred feet away! You can imagine what an impression this tragedy made on me as a young child.

It was clear to us that we had an obligation to this Scottish family whose journey had been interrupted on our very doorstep. A traumatic event had claimed most of their possessions. They were stuck in the middle of Africa without transportation. They had no idea what to do.

The Rickett family had some decisions to make, and they needed a safe haven to rest while they made those decisions.

The Christian thing to do was to provide dinner and overnight accommodations in our home for our unexpected guests. Everybody in our family moved over to make room for them. Dad and Mom even gave their bedroom to the Scottish couple.

One overnight became two. A week passed. Two weeks. The Ricketts ended up staying through Christmas, and left shortly after New Year's to hitch-hike across the Sahara Desert and move on toward home.

We met a critical need for our guests until they could make decisions about what to do. In the process we made some new friends, friends with whom we had the privilege of sharing the Gospel. Although I do not know if they ever trusted Jesus for their salvation, God got their attention.

Bob Rickett concluded, "God brought us all the way into the heart of Africa and forced us to stop at your door. He must have brought us here for *some* reason." We think we know what that reason was!

By the way, the Rickett family arrived home safely. Dad and Mom kept in touch with them by letter, and even visited them in Scotland some years later. Mom reports that Ruby Rickett still writes her "at least once a year," especially at Christmas.

3

WHAT'S FOR DINNER?

Wanted: Missionary Hunters

I n the 1950's, animals were plentiful and poaching (illegal hunting) had not become the curse it is today. In those days, missionaries provided almost all the meat for their tables by hunting. It was not unusual for even missionary women to contribute in this way. Several missionary ladies were noted for their hunting prowess.

Of course missionaries always licensed their guns and paid all the required fees for animals they chose to kill.

Sometimes local authorities contacted a missionary hunter, asking him to help the community by killing a rogue elephant which was endangering their villages and devastating their gardens.

When a missionary killed an animal for an African church conference, of course the kill provided meat for all those attending the conference.

If the kill was for personal use, the missionary hunter would ordinarily select the portion of meat he preferred to take home with him. He would take only what he knew his family could eat before it spoiled. The heat wouldn't allow meat to be kept long, and the missionaries' kerosene refrigerators had such small freezer compartments that they offered very little help.

The missionary hunter either designated the rest of the meat for the local pastor and church people, or offered it to be shared by the villagers. People in nearby villages often profited from the kill.

Believe me, in those days hunting served as an effective tool for "friendship evangelism." The villagers were always happy to have missionaries living nearby, especially if these messengers of the Gospel had a gun and knew how to use it!

Cape buffalo Dad shot, Kyabe area, mid 1950s
Left to right: Dad, Larry, Tom and Tim

Two American hunters for whom Dad served as guide, with the elephant they shot, Kyabe area, mid 1950s

The Elephant Dad Shot

Through the years, among other things, Dad shot antelope of all varieties, warthog, leopard, hyena, hippo, giraffe, ostrich, cape buffalo and even elephant.

One day when I was about five years old, Dad shot a full-grown elephant not far behind our house. With our three oldest siblings all away at school at the time, Tim, Tom, Dale and I were the only kids left at home.

Early one afternoon, Dad drove into the yard and brought the pickup to an abrupt stop in a cloud of dust. "Hey, boys!" he called excitedly. "Do you want to see an elephant? I just killed an elephant, only about three kilometers behind the mission! You'll probably never be able to see an elephant closer to home than this." Of course, we excitedly piled into the back of the truck to go see!

We followed the dirt "two-track" road (a road consisting of a dirt path for each set of wheels to follow, with grass growing up in the unused middle of the road) behind the mission property for several kilometers. When Dad pulled off to the side and shut off the engine, we heard what sounded like the babble and chatter of an open market, with people everywhere promoting their wares and dickering for the best price. We wouldn't have needed Dad to show us the way; we could have simply followed the noise! Nevertheless, we followed Dad through the grass and trees to witness a never-to-be-forgotten sight.

How they had gathered so quickly I cannot explain. People from all over the surrounding region had either heard the shot or received the news from someone. They all came assuming the best. They came carrying their metal or plastic pails, their large aluminum basins, their homemade hatchets and hunting knives. They came expecting to cash in on this bounty, to return home with meat for their hungry families.

The elephant was lying on its right side, with its four feet toward us. Dad allowed us kids to crawl all over the fallen elephant, while the villagers tried to be patient. Dad had made the kill, so the polite thing to do was wait for him.

Given permission finally to start the butchering, some of the men took the lead, slicing through the tough skin and subcutaneous layers of fat the length of the elephant's belly.

Halted by the rib cage, they hacked through the sternum with their hatchets and, finally, prying back and breaking off one rib after another, they began to cut out anything they could reach. The stomach and intestines were first. Of course blood was everywhere, coating the limp, slimy folds of flesh and strings of entrails. The heavy smell of blood mixed with the stink of partially digested food and excrement.

Fascinated and horrified at the same time, we watched as now several men pried open the elephant's rib cage and one brave man crawled inside the abdominal cavity. Disappearing from view, he continued the butchering on behalf of the waiting crowd gathered around the carcass. From time to time his bloody hand would appear to extend another tasty morsel. *There, that's the liver. Here comes a portion of the heart. Those are the kidneys. That must be a lung.* And there were more intestines – what seemed like miles of them!

Each morsel was snatched up by eager hands, the meat to be later cleaned, cooked and finally – *finally* – consumed with great appreciation. These people would eat meat today, a rare enough treat for people whose usual diet consisted of the standard manioc paste and leaf greens, along with the occasional piece of tropical fruit or ear of roasted field corn.

As the butchering continued, we realized that by the time they were done, there would be nothing left but skin and bones. These people knew how to use a dead animal to good advantage. Nothing usable would be wasted!

But we would not remain until the job was done. As the successful hunter, Dad could choose the portion of the animal he wanted. He chose, and the rest of the animal could be divided up any way the villagers wanted.

Elephant Trunk Steaks

The portion of the downed elephant that Dad chose was its trunk. Yes, the *trunk*.

I'm still not sure what made Dad choose the elephant's trunk. However, there may have been some logic to his decision. While the trunk is a muscle, it is nevertheless somewhat mottled with fat. Cooking it, you might therefore expect it to be more tender than, for example, a piece of elephant rump steak!

Dad arranged for some men to carry the elephant trunk out to the road for us and load it into our pickup. Thinking back on this, I can't remember how many men helped us. Obviously one man couldn't have done it by himself. Two probably wouldn't be sufficient – for either they would manage the two ends and allow the middle to drag on the ground, or they would manage the middle and allow the two ends to drag. I think the job must have required three men.

The elephant trunk was laid lengthwise in the eight-foot bed of the pickup. My three brothers and I took our places in the back with that heavy piece of meat, standing on the floor of the truck bed and holding on to the wooden side rails of the rack. As we moved down the uneven dirt road back toward the mission, tilting in and out of the ever-present ruts, we found that the elephant trunk wanted to roll to one side of the truck bed, then back to the other side.

So we were careful to call out a warning to each other: "It's coming your way, Tim – save yourself!"

"Get up out of its way, Tom – it's coming!"

"Watch out, Dale, it's rolling toward you! Don't let it crush you!"

Safely back at the mission, we wondered what Mom and Dad would *do* with the elephant's trunk. We didn't have to wonder long.

An African man helped to butcher the trunk. He used a sharp knife to slice lengthwise through the thick covering of the trunk, and began to skin that piece of muscle meat by running the knife between the skin and the flesh a bit at a time and peeling back the skin. Finally the skin lay off to one side, and all that was left was a long, slimy, bloody mass of "meat."

What else do you need to do to make an elephant trunk ready to eat? Well, I know it's gross to talk about it, but . . . this is the elephant's nose, and it has nostrils. Long nostrils. Two very long nostrils. A lot of . . . *stuff* . . . can hide in there! *How do you go about cleaning out an elephant's trunk?* I can't really say that our butcher "hosed out" the nostrils of the trunk for, in fact, we didn't even *own* such a thing as a garden hose! Somehow he flushed out the nostrils, but I don't remember how he did it.

Next, from either end of the trunk, the African man's sharp knife was used to slice elephant trunk steaks of manageable size.

That day, we enjoyed all the meat we could eat! Some of the steaks were adult-size, as they were cut from the larger, upper end of the trunk. Each of these steaks filled the frying pan and nearly covered a dinner plate. Each of the children received a smaller steak, cut from the smaller, tapered tip of the trunk. Still a good size, our steaks left just a bit of room on our plates for other food.

But why would we *need* extra space on the plate for other food? Each elephant trunk steak had two holes in it – one for the rice and one for the peas!

4

LEAVING HOME TO GO TO SCHOOL

Now It Was My Turn!

During the years I was growing up as a missionary kid in central Africa, going to school meant leaving home. You may react by saying, "Of *course*, you had to leave home. Even in the United States, anyone who goes to school leaves his house to go spend his day where the school is located." No, I mean that (for MKs living in primitive places like Africa) going to school meant *really leaving home!*

Missionary mothers took the responsibility of teaching their young children kindergarten and first grade. Then at the age of seven, the children would leave home to attend an MK boarding school. That was my experience, along with many other MKs around the world.

BMM had established such a boarding school at *Crampel* (later renamed *Kaga Bandoro*), in what became the Central African Republic, in order to provide for the educational needs of its missionary families in the heart of Africa. This elementary school, named Milner Memorial School, handled between fifteen and thirty missionary kids at a time, from second grade through eighth grade, in a one-room school setting.

BMM's school at Crampel *for missionary children,*
2nd – 8th grades all in one classroom, early 50s?

While a few of the school kids lived with their parents there at *Crampel*, most of them lived in the dormitory built for this purpose. In the middle of the long, one-story dorm building, the dorm-parents' bedroom was connected to a large communal living room, dining room and kitchen. This huge central area of the dorm separated the boys' end of the dormitory and the girls' end. Each end contained a number of bedrooms and a couple of communal bathrooms. Each of the dorm's bedrooms was equipped with three or four sets of bunk beds and a multitude of simple homemade dressers.

A missionary couple was assigned as the dorm-parents for the MKs entrusted to them. This couple committed to love, nurture and train this ready-made family as they would their own children.

Of course, managing a dormitory with so many children required a clearly-understood set of rules. And those rules had to be enforced in order to keep things under control. As you would expect, when trying to maintain discipline, the challenge was how to do it with love and consistency.

The Crampel *dormitory in later years, late 60s?*

It was to this MK boarding school and to this dormitory that I went with excitement at the age of seven. Finally, I was old enough to do what big kids did and I was eager to get on with it! I had watched older MKs and even some of my older siblings go away to school at the magic age of seven. Now it was my turn!

Having a brother or sister already at the boarding school, or a best friend going to school at the same time, made this major transition a lot easier for a young MK. My sister, Maribeth, was returning to school for eighth grade, and my twin brothers, Tim and Tom, were returning for fourth grade. So I had three siblings with me as I went away to school for the first time at the age of seven.

The Realities of Life

From then on, all through elementary school, I spent eight months of every year away from my parents: four months at school for the fall semester, one month at home for Christmas vacation, again four months at school, then three months at home for summer vacation. For four months at a time, we didn't see our parents. The only communication we had with them was by postal mail, for there were no phones nor email available to us in central Africa in those days. But this was the way life *was* . . . . I decided I might as well accept it and make the best of it.

Over time, quality boarding schools similar to BMM's school at *Crampel* were set up as necessary by various mission agencies, particularly in the more primitive parts of the world, as they took responsibility for the educational needs of their missionary families. The trend started with elementary schools but high schools soon followed.

In those days, *how* else *would missionary parents provide an adequate education for their children in such a primitive place?* There were no other good options to be considered at that time. In such a backward part of the world, any local school was woefully and hopelessly inadequate in terms of facilities, equipment, curriculum, teacher qualifications and preparation for future entrance into the American school system – not to speak of the security issues involved! And at that time, there were no correspondence school or home-school options available to help the missionary teacher-mom.

So both parents and children made some unusual sacrifices and tried to accept them as realities of life.

I Didn't Know I Was to Be Pitied

Don't get me wrong – I wasn't thrilled about being separated from my parents. But one child after another, Mom and Dad had been preparing us mentally and emotionally for this day. The circumstances of my MK life were accepted without self-pity and without rebellion.

I didn't know I was to be pitied as an MK for the sorry life I had to endure until, during our next furlough, well-meaning ladies in the churches would pat me on the head, shaking their heads sadly and murmuring their comforting words: "You poor little boy. Having to live in Africa and, now, having to go away to boarding school . . . "

I desperately tried to understand, but failed. You see, I *loved* living in Africa. In fact, I pitied those children who *couldn't* live in Africa and experience the adventures I was privileged to enjoy!

*"You **Have** to Cry Hard Like That"*

When missionary parents dropped off their children at *Crampel* for a new four-month school term, they were usually very careful to keep their goodbyes short. How could parents manage this heart-rending situation?

Steel yourselves . . . .

Say a brief goodbye, trying to control your emotions so you can keep your child from breaking into ragged sobs . . . .

Now drive off quickly to avoid letting your child watch your own emotional meltdown.

Of course some MKs did cry inconsolably until, exhausted, they finally allowed themselves to be comforted. Others cried sincerely but briefly, then turned happily enough to other activities.

I remember one MK, however, who knew how to work the system. She said goodbye to her parents with the obligatory hugs and kisses, and cried the obligatory tears like her fragile heart was breaking – until she saw their truck disappear from sight onto the main road. At that moment she wiped her tears away, grinned at her well-intended deception and announced to all of us within earshot, "You *have* to cry hard like that when your parents leave. They want you to show them you're real sad when they go. If you don't cry hard, then *they'll* be sad!"

The Positives Outweighed the Negatives

My own MK experience has been very positive. But not all MKs share my point of view – for their circumstances have somehow been very different from mine.

Separation from one's parents in a boarding school will never be an ideal situation for any child. In *my* case, I thrived. I became more independent. I believe I am stronger today because of it.

I don't blame my parents for anything. I know they made the best decisions they could for my good.

But at the same time I am very thankful that there *are* other educational alternatives available to missionary parents today. What an advantage we have today! Careful choices about schooling for our MKs, combined with good parenting, should lead to less trauma for MKs in the future. I pray that will be true.

To be sure, not all of my experiences were positive. But for me, the positives far outweighed the negatives.

Tapioca and Bread Pudding

One not-so-fond memory of my dormitory experience at boarding school was being forced to eat the desserts. Each child in the dormitory had to stay at the table until his food was finished, including his dessert.

Ordinarily I would not resist eating dessert. Anybody who knows me knows there's not much I don't enjoy eating, and I love desserts!

But our dorm-parents must have found a special sale on tapioca pudding in bulk. We had it served to us so often that we got sick of it! And bread pudding – many of us developed a powerful dislike for the stuff.

Yet we were forced to sit there at the table until our portions were gone.

Over time, certain MKs developed inventive and elaborate ways of dispensing with their desserts without having to taste any more of it than was absolutely necessary! For example, they learned to move the offending dessert into a napkin or a pocket, bit by bit, with great patience. Of course the goal was to accomplish the process without attracting any unwanted attention that might bring their deception to a premature conclusion.

These were the same deceptions practiced by the same MKs to get rid of other wholesome foods, like the mushy and totally inedible canned peas served occasionally with dinner.

There were several MKs who excelled in this practice. Their identities are known to some of us who caught on to their tricks during our years at the dorm. But any effort to worm the information out of us will be unsuccessful. Our brotherhood is solid. There isn't one of us who will give them up.

For the sake of nutrition and health, I can understand being forced to eat the main meal. But *dessert?* I have a hard time eating tapioca and bread pudding to this day! And I have discovered something interesting: a number of other MKs who were with me in the dorm during those years struggle likewise with those same "delicacies" today!

Precious Memories

One of the reasons I was so eager to go to boarding school was because there I would have lots of other MKs to play with – not just my siblings. I *wanted* to go! There were about thirty MKs at *Crampel* while I was there. Although certain kids became my special friends, they all became like brothers and sisters to me.

Special activities on Friday evenings provided many delightful memories – memories that cause me to smile even now! Many Friday evenings, the MKs had an occasion to get out of the dorm. Divided into smaller groups, we were invited by other missionaries stationed at *Crampel* to spend the evening with them. They took special care to prepare for us a wonderful meal and a great evening of games and fun. This became a highlight of the week for us.

Once a month, our Friday evening activity was a "Skit Night." Hilarious fun characterized each of these occasions, as MKs (and sometimes adults) prepared their skits to present to the group. This was a big deal for the MKs. We always ended up with a full and satisfying program of comic readings, dramatic renditions of fairy tales and skits that made good fun of one another or played tricks on some unfortunate person!

One year a favorite series of plays that continued from one Skit Night to another was the enactment of a number of events drawn from the legend of "Brer Rabbit." The fun was in how this cunning character always managed to outwit his mortal enemies, Brer Bear and Brer Fox. I had the distinct honor of landing the highly-desired role of Brer Rabbit. After all, I was the one who had the idea for the skit, the one who recruited and organized others to help me . . . and the one who made all the decisions about who would play which character! Undoubtedly, this desired role was the one that launched my distinguished acting career.

The dormitory occupied one end of the *Crampel* mission property, along with a playground with swings and merry-go-round, a miniature golf course (during some of my years at the dorm) and an elementary-school-sized softball field. The softball outfield was limited by a home-run fence. What a victory it was to hit an occasional home-run "out of the park"!

During a couple of my upper elementary years at the dormitory, the MKs participated in an active softball league designed especially for them. We were divided into three or four teams. Believe me, we took this very seriously! Team names were finally chosen after lengthy debate – the name chosen by our team was the "Colts." Colorful team flags were designed and displayed with pride. The competition between teams was fierce. Our win-loss records were tracked with great care. The end-of-season tournament each school term was an occasion for team pride, high spirits and passionate play. Prizes were given to the winning team.

Because of the close relationship between our BMM missionaries on the field, MKs in central Africa were taught to call all adult missionaries by the title "Uncle" or "Aunt." In many ways, they filled a void in our lives, serving as satisfying replacements for our real uncles and aunts in the US, relatives who were now unavailable to us.

I have good memories of dorm-parents Uncle LaVerne and Aunt Beulah Olson, Uncle Bill and Aunt Betty Vander-ground and Uncle Ben and Aunt Nina Kendrick. I loved them all, but the Olsons have a special place in my heart, because it was Aunt Beulah who led me to the Lord.

5

"IF YOU WERE TO DIE TONIGHT . . ."

Always the Same Question

"Are you sure you're saved? If you were to die tonight, do you know for sure you would go to heaven?" That was the question my older sister, Maribeth, insisted on asking me every night before I went to the boys' end of the dorm to go to bed.

Maribeth had three younger brothers with her at boarding school that year. I had just turned seven years old and I was in my first term at school. My twin brothers, Tim and Tom, would have been eight years old, almost nine. Maribeth, being a few years older, took her responsibility as older sister very seriously. Our mother wasn't around, so Maribeth believed it was her duty to act in Mom's place to "mother" us.

Every evening before bedtime, our dorm-parents called all the MKs together for evening devotions. After devotions, Maribeth said good-night to her three younger brothers before letting us go to bed.

One night early in the term, while Tim and Tom moved off toward the boys' end of the dorm, Maribeth held me back and asked me, "Are you sure you're saved? If you were to die tonight, do you know for sure you would go to heaven?"

"Yes, I know I'm saved."

The next night, Maribeth held me back again and asked the same question.

Evening devotions in the Crampel *dorm, late 1950s*
Tom and Tim in back row

"Yes," I answered again. "I'm sure I would go to heaven."

This became a nightly occurrence, as Maribeth asked me over and over again, "Larry, are you really sure that you're saved?" Always the same question.

My answer was always the same. "Yes, Maribeth, I'm *sure!*" I became impatient with her persistent nagging. I couldn't understand what could be lacking in my life that had Maribeth concerned that I might not be saved.

I knew all about Jesus, that He is the Son of God and the Savior of the world, that He had come into the world to provide for my eternal salvation through His sacrifice on the cross. In fact, I *believed* what I understood from the Bible about Jesus. I understood the truth about my sinfulness, and I think I could have told you how a person can be saved.

Further, our parents were missionaries. We attended all the church meetings with them. Of course, they led us to pray for all our meals. They directed our daily time of family devotions, when we read a portion from the Bible and prayed together as a family. In fact, Dad taught us early in our lives to develop a habit of *personal* devotions, reading at least a few verses and praying by ourselves.

"If anybody could be sure of going to heaven," I thought, "it would be me!"

But my sister's often-repeated question began to bother me. "If you were to die tonight, do you know for sure you would go to heaven?" Why – *why?* – did Maribeth think I might not be saved? God the Holy Spirit was working in my heart to convict me of my spiritual need.

I Had Never **Done** *This*

Late one Sunday evening in November 1958, Maribeth approached me again with her usual question: "Do you know for sure you will go to heaven if you were to die tonight?"

This time my response was not one of impatience and denial of my need. Suddenly I surprised myself by breaking into tears. I sobbed, "No, I'm *not* sure." Finally I understood that, though I knew all the right information and believed what the Bible said about Jesus, I had never become a child of God by accepting Jesus for myself as my Savior! I had never *done* this.

"Do you want to be sure tonight? You can trust Jesus tonight as your Savior."

"Yes," I choked out. "I want to do that tonight."

Twelve-year-old Maribeth had been faithful in prodding me to recognize my personal need of Christ. Now she took me to see our dorm-mother, Aunt Beulah. Of course, she was delighted to help me settle the matter of my salvation!

My Greatest Adventure Ever

I followed Aunt Beulah outside to sit on the brick veranda in front of the dormitory. In the darkness of the African night, we could see the stars twinkling in the cloudless skies above. Gently, she asked me about my desire to trust Christ as my Savior.

Turning her Bible toward the single bare light bulb hanging over the front door of the dorm, Aunt Beulah asked me to read John 3:16: "For God so loved the world that He gave His only begotten Son, that whoever believes in Him should not perish but have everlasting life."

Seeking to make this personal to me, Aunt Beulah put my name into the verse: "For God so loved Larry Fogle that He gave His only begotten Son, that if Larry Fogle believes in Him, Larry Fogle would not perish, but Larry Fogle would have everlasting life." Now I understood that God didn't only love the world in general – He loved everybody in the world individually. That meant *me*! God loved me personally, and to demonstrate His love He sent His Son to die for my sin. Now it was up to me to personally place my faith in Jesus as *my* Savior.

Aunt Beulah continued by asking me to read the next verses, John 3:17-18: "For God did not send His Son into the world to condemn the world, but that the world through Him might be saved. He who believes in Him is not condemned; but he who does not believe is condemned already, because he has not believed in the name of the only begotten Son of God."

Two categories of people are described in these verses – those who are not condemned and those who are condemned already. The difference between them is that one has believed in Jesus, and the other has not. Believing in Jesus is what frees us from the judgment of God that we deserve because of our sin.

"Condemned or not condemned . . . In which of the two categories are you, Larry?"

"It says until I believe in Jesus, I'm still condemned," I answered with a child's simple understanding. The verse was so clear.

I now understood that it wasn't enough to believe *about* Jesus; I had to believe *in* Him. And that Sunday evening, under the starlit African sky, Aunt Beulah led me to pray a simple prayer in which I claimed Jesus as my own personal Savior and my Lord.

Now Aunt Beulah asked, "Did you just believe in Jesus?"

"Yes," came my firm answer.

"So, condemned or not condemned . . . In which of the two categories are you *now*?"

How proudly I exclaimed, "I'm not condemned any more!"

Not condemned. Thank you, Mom and Dad, for your teaching. Thank you, Maribeth, for your prodding. Thank you, Aunt Beulah, for your guidance. And thank You, Jesus, for Your salvation.

6

A MISSIONARY KID ON FURLOUGH

Where is "Home"?

"Home" . . . What does that mean for an MK? Most of us MKs struggle a bit with that issue.

When well-meaning people ask an MK, "Where is home for you?" do they mean your home on the mission field, or your home in the United States? Are they asking about the place where you were born? Where you live most of the time? Where you currently live? Where most of your relatives are? Where you go to school? Where your family lives during furlough? It seems that the list of options goes on and on.

As an American citizen, the US was my *home* country. I was proud to call the US home. But as an MK, I belonged to a family that had also claimed Chad, our *host* country, as our home.

Some MKs love their home country so much that they may hate leaving to go to the mission field. They might tend to resist calling their host country their home.

On the other hand, other MKs may develop such a deep attachment to their host country, the country to which God has called their family to serve, that they hate leaving to return to their home country. Why? It doesn't feel like home any more.

I don't believe either of these two extremes is healthy. The ideal situation is one in which the MK loves both his home country *and* his host country. If he loves both, I would guess that the likelihood of emotional or spiritual estrangement in the life of the MK might be minimized.

I had two homes. Chad was my home – where I was born and where as a child I lived most of the time. But the US was also my home – where my relatives lived, and where we lived for a year at a time on furlough.

As a child I was clearly more attached to Chad, because I had spent so little time in the US. Having been born in Chad, I was only three years old when I experienced my first furlough with the family in the US. I do not have any clear memories of the US until we returned for furlough when I was eight, ready for fourth grade. Naturally I was more attached to Chad than to the US. Chad, my host country, was home for me and I loved living in Africa.

But I also came to love the US as my home country. I still do today. If anything, the twenty-five years I have lived outside of the US have increased my appreciation for this wonderful country!

Going Home to the US

Going home . . . What did that mean to this MK who loved both his home country and his host country? It depended on where I was at the time. When I was in the US, I looked forward to going home to Chad. When I was in Chad, it was exciting to think about getting back on a plane and going home to the US!

When it was time for furlough, our family looked forward to returning to the US where we could get away from the pressures of the missionary work for a time (typically a year). During this time, we would renew relationships with our family and friends in the US, report to our supporting churches and restore our physical health and energy.

One of the things we enjoyed about going home to the US for furlough was the travel itself. How many kids who live in the US got to travel as much as we did? Back and forth we went through the years, from Africa to the US then back again.

I don't remember at all my first trip to the US at the age of three. At the end of that furlough, when I was four, I have faint memories of our family traveling back to Africa by boat – a passenger ship called the *Queen Elizabeth.*

In life jackets during safety drill on Queen Elizabeth, *1955*
Left to right: Front row – Larry, Tim, Tom; Second row – Maribeth, Mom, Dale

All our travel in my later childhood years was done by propeller airplane. I remember the loud, throbbing engines . . . the severe earaches caused by the changes in air pressure . . . the almost-every-time airsickness. In spite of those things, each overseas trip was exciting!

For About the Same Price

Traveling by plane between the US and Africa always took us through Europe. The plane tickets were always expensive. For about the same price, one could fly through Paris, London, or even Rome. And once the airport connection was determined, it would cost very little more to spend a few days in that location to do some sight-seeing. The only additional cost to us for that interruption in our flight schedule would be our carefully-managed personal expenses for the days we spent there.

On our way to the US for furlough (or on our way back to Africa again) – thanks to our parents' advance planning – our family experienced some exotic places! I don't remember much about Madrid, Spain, or Lisbon, Portugal, where we visited when I was very young. In Paris, France, we were fascinated by the *Eiffel Tower*, the *Notre Dame Cathedral* and the famous *Louvre Museum*. In London, England, my favorite memories are riding on a double-decker bus and visiting the lifelike *Madame Tussaud's Wax Museum*. In Rome, Italy, our sightseeing included the *Vatican* and *Saint Peter's Cathedral*, the *Roman Coliseum* and a memorable visit to the *Catacombs*.

When going home to the US for furlough, such a stop in Europe gave our family a few days of breathing space – an intermission – between the hectic days of packing and closing out ministries in Africa and, upon arrival in the US, the emotional days of seeing dear friends again and facing the social and cultural expectations of our home country.

"Can I Go Play Now?"

Furlough gave us the opportunity to reconnect with our relatives. I didn't know them very well. How could I, when I saw them so seldom? I was much closer to the missionaries in central Africa, people whom I saw more often. To me these missionaries were "Uncle Bob and Aunt Vera," "Uncle Gene and Aunt Millie," "Uncle Ted and Aunt Lila," "Uncle Dave and Aunt Ruth," and others. But I could hardly remember the names of my real uncles and aunts in the US!

In family reunions and on other occasions when we saw our relatives, I struggled to recognize uncles and aunts. It was easier to remember those who had loaned our family a used black-and-white television or who had done something else special for us. Sometimes I was introduced to a cousin whom I was sure I had never even met before.

During our first furlough after I was born, Grandma McCuen visited our house. I was three or four at the time. I had heard about grandmas and grandpas – *other* people had grandparents – but I never knew mine. Mom's parents were the only grandparents I had left. Yet for some reason I have no memories at all of Grandpa; although he lived for a few more years, none of us younger kids remember him at all. And Grandma was actually my step-grandma – Mom's step-mother, since her widowed father had remarried. This visit from Grandma was my first opportunity to meet one of my grandparents.

Escorted into Grandma's presence, I was introduced to her. "Say hello to Grandma McCuen, Larry."

"Hello, Grandma," I parroted politely. She seemed quite nice and said something to me in response. When she paused I hesitated, not knowing what else was expected of me. Then I turned to Mom, asking, "Can I go play now?"

That was my brief acquaintance with my step-grandma. I don't remember ever meeting her again.

A Blur of Confused Images

Our furloughs were always a blur of confused images. While we had a home in Mishawaka, Indiana, and went to church and school in the same town, we spent a lot of time in the car, moving around the country so that our parents could report to our supporting churches.

There was no way to avoid the extensive travel that furlough required. There were months when each Sunday found us in a different church. This often meant staying overnight with some family of the church who offered us their kind hospitality. Of course, we had to be on our best behavior! We needed to be flexible enough to accept different sleeping arrangements everywhere, and compliant enough to obey any rules that were specific to that home.

In each church we found new friends. However, the excitement of making new friends at the beginning of the weekend was somehow diminished when we had to say goodbye only a day or two later. We knew that we might never see them again.

People who leave the US to live in other countries, including missionaries and their MKs, often face severe cultural adjustments. They usually find themselves in a place very different from the US. It may be a place where the scenery and climate are unfamiliar. The race, skin color, language, dress and foods of the people may be different from what the newcomers have ever experienced before. The social and cultural expectations they face in their new host country may throw them into a state of confusion and frustration that we call "culture shock."

It is also true that missionaries and MKs returning to the US for furlough may face "reverse culture shock." Over time they have finally made the necessary adjustments in their lives on the mission field, and that has become "home" for them. Now they must adjust *back* to the expectations of life in the US!

For an MK, fitting into an American school and figuring out how to act in a way that would be considered "normal" by American kids is a challenge that must be faced again every furlough. Although I was fairly out-going, I always wanted to avoid calling undesirable attention to myself. I certainly didn't want to earn a reputation for being weird! At the same time I held myself to a higher standard than most kids in the US, and would not compromise too much to fit in with the crowd.

Furlough was a good experience for me. I enjoyed the new experiences which constantly presented themselves. People were interested to hear about Africa. People were very nice to us everywhere we went. But from the standpoint of a child, those furloughs seemed like a blur of movement. Even today I find it a bit difficult to focus my thoughts on any one event during those furloughs.

An Old, Two-Story House

I was too young to remember where we lived during my first furlough in Mishawaka, when I was three, but I do remember our house during those furloughs when I was eight and twelve. Dad and Mom had bought an old two-story house on Battell Street. We lived there when we were in the US, and others rented the house when we were overseas.

My two oldest siblings, Lois and Phil, had lived with the family only for the first four years of my life; schooling separated them from the family from that time on. So during my second and third furloughs in the US, there were only seven of us to share the three-bedroom house on Battell Street.

Our parents used the bedroom on the main floor of the old house. The four of us brothers (Tim, Tom, Larry and Dale) were crammed into one of the bedrooms upstairs, occupying two sets of bunks – it was always bunk beds and cramped quarters, at home as well as in the dormitory. Maribeth reveled in the unspeakable luxury of having the other upstairs bedroom all to herself, never showing a speck of sympathy for her unfortunate brothers!

Our smaller family back in US for furlough, 1959
Left to right: Tim, Dad, Maribeth, Larry, Dale, Mom, Tom

"Three in the Same Grade?*"*

In the MK school in Africa I had moved through second and third grades in one year, ending up in the same grade as my twin brothers, Tim and Tom. Now we were to attend fourth grade at Battell School at the end of our block. (Dale may also have been enrolled, several years behind us in school.)

When Dad and Mom walked down to the school with us to talk to the principal, the conversation made us laugh!

"These are the children we want to enroll in your school: Tim, Tom and Larry."

"Well, we will be delighted to have several of your family in our school! How about Tim – what grade is he in?"

"Fourth grade."

"All right, what about Tom?"

"Well, Tim and Tom are twins, so Tom is in fourth, just like Tim."

"And the younger one, Larry? Which grade is he in?'

"He is also in fourth. He moved through the younger grades quickly and ended up in the same grade as the twins."

"What? Three in the *same grade*? You are kidding!" The principal was astounded to hear that in his school there would be three of us boys from the same family in fourth grade that year! He concluded by joking, "If you had *another* child in the same grade, we would have to give you a 'home room' to yourselves!"

A Church with a Missionary Legacy

From our house, we had to walk only one and a half city blocks to our church. Even as a child, I appreciated our home church, First Baptist Church of Mishawaka, Indiana.

Our church enjoyed quite a missionary legacy. From its own congregation, First Baptist Church sent out some of the pioneer Baptist Mid-Missions missionaries to central Africa – and other missionaries since. During the early history of the Mission, this church also served as the BMM headquarters.

Dr. Roy Hamman, formerly a missionary himself in French Equatorial Africa, was our pastor throughout my childhood years. He is the one who baptized me during one furlough when I was twelve. I had the greatest respect for him.

Looking back, I would describe Pastor Hamman as a man of great personal dignity, genuine love for people, passion for God's work, careful handling of God's Word and discerning counsel. I did not realize until much later how powerful was the influence of this godly leader on my life, shaping my view of the ministry and what a pastor should be like.

Our church was a well-established church, full of godly people who were serious about their service in the church. As missionaries overseas, our family was in the US only one year out of every five, but that occasional furlough year allowed many of the folks in our church to positively impact my young life.

A Family Vacation to Remember

An outstanding memory Dad and Mom created for our family one furlough was a road trip through the western US. The trip was planned to combine visits with relatives in a couple of western states, meetings in several churches out that direction and some never-to-be-forgotten vacation time with the family.

If I remember correctly, this trip happened in early summer 1964 when I was thirteen, just before Dad and Mom returned to Africa for yet another term. We needed this special family time, for we were facing a major separation.

Lois, my oldest sister, had finished her nurses' training and had been married to Jerry for several years.

Phil, my oldest brother, had finished college and his ROTC training as an army officer. His military obligations were already occupying his time and, besides, he was to be married to Betty in August.

The next oldest in the family, Maribeth, was busy with plans for her own wedding to Don. She was to be married in early August, just a week before Phil!

Of course, Lois, Phil and Maribeth would all be unable to join us on our road trip through the west.

Tim, Tom and I would remain in the US for high school when Dad and Mom headed back overseas at the end of the summer. Dale would accompany our parents, to stay with them a couple of years until he would also have to return to the US for high school.

The family would be splitting in so many different directions that fall, the separation could potentially be more traumatic than normal – for everyone, but especially for the younger ones.

So a special family trip was in order for those of the family who could join us.

The whole family wouldn't have fit anyway in the 1964 Chevrolet Biscayne provided by a supporting church for our use that furlough. I guess it was a good thing that the oldest three kids *couldn't* come with us! The four of us younger boys would be the ones to enjoy the trip.

We had already spent more than our fair share of time that furlough in the white, four-door sedan. So you might wonder how willing we were to climb back in the car again. But we were excited about this trip – it was *vacation*!

Yes, our vacation trip included some church meetings and the necessary "come-say-hello-to-your-relatives" visits with uncles and aunts and cousins whose names we sometimes didn't even remember. But in addition, among other things, this road trip through the western US allowed us to see the *Rocky Mountains*, *Yellowstone National Park*, the *Oregon Trail Interpretive Center*, *Crater Lake National Park*, a forest of petrified redwoods and the *Grand Canyon*.

We drove into *Yellowstone* after dark in a snow blizzard – and this was July! We found the cabin that had been reserved for us, but had nothing with which to make a fire in the fireplace so we all froze that night.

That trip through the west made us appreciate the US all the more – its vastness, its variety, its beauty. Because of that trip, for example, *Crater Lake* will always be for me one of the most beautiful places on earth. In addition, it gave us the special family time we needed – truly, a family vacation to remember!

7

HIGH SCHOOL IN THE US: 1964 – 1968

A Heart-Rending Decision

T he MK boarding school in Central African Republic continued only through eighth grade. Missionaries with children entering their high school years were forced to face a heart-rending decision. If they did not make arrangements for their children to stay with others in the US to allow them to continue their schooling, these missionaries would have to leave the mission field to which God had called them.

Some missionary parents found a good situation for their children with loving relatives or dear friends from their church. Others, like our own parents, chose to take advantage of a boarding home for high-school-age MKs that had been set up earlier by Baptist Mid-Missions to meet this very need.

Lois, Phil and Maribeth had all lived at this boarding home through their high-school years. In our turn Tim, Tom and I were now going together to live there, and Dale would join us at a later time.

Our parents got the three of us boys settled at "Mid-Maples" in time for our freshman year of high school before they returned overseas. We would live in that home during our four years of high school, from 1964-1968. We would not see Dad and Mom again until our high school graduation.

Tom, Larry, Dale, Tim facing high-school years, early 1964

None of us would have wished to be separated from our parents, but we knew God had called them to serve Him in Africa. We would not have wanted them to be disobedient to His call. Any pain we suffered from this separation was certainly no more than the pain Dad and Mom suffered as they left their children behind.

Mid-Maples

It was easy to see why BMM's boarding home for MKs was called "Mid-Maples." Occupying a couple of acres in the outskirts of Wheaton, Illinois, the oversized, two-story house was surrounded by stately, shady, maple trees. The huge, park-like front yard gave us plenty of room to play a casual game of football or hit a softball around, while the smaller back yard was good for all kinds of other activities. The long driveway gave way to a large, black-topped area in front of the garages, where we could play basketball when we wanted.

"Mid-Maples" – the home for MKs where all seven kids
in our family spent at least some of their high-school years

To those passing by on the road, the overall appearance of the grand old house set among the mature maples was that of a well-kept estate.

The house itself boasted a large master suite, at least five other bed-rooms and three other baths, two massive rooms used as living room and dining room, an industrial-size kitchen, a screened sun-porch at the back and a porch that ran the length of the front of the house. The basement provided plenty of storage space, plus laundry and utilities.

The number of teens living at Mid-Maples each year that I was there varied between twelve and fifteen. Of course, guys and girls lived on different floors. There were fewer bedrooms on the main floor and therefore less bunk beds. *Which* floor we lived on each year depended on the number of guys and girls who would live there that year.

Can you imagine living together in one house with a dozen other teenagers (even if it *was* a large house)? To live year-round with a bunch of teen-agers you personally choose to be your companions would be one thing. Imagine having to put up with a random mix of teens for a year – including some whom you might never choose as your best friends!

Our MK family changed from year to year. Most of these MKs loved the things of God, but others loved the things of the world. Some were proud of their missionary heritage; a few, however, were bitter about their experience. Most of them were cooperative and obedient, while several were rebellious. Most wanted to take a committed stand for the Lord Jesus, but there were those who were willing to do anything to blend with the crowd and be popular. The majority were pleasant and good-natured; a few were hard, unhappy and angry – tension marked all their relationships.

It took a special missionary couple to cope with all those teenagers during these formative and volatile years of their lives. This couple would serve not only as house-parents, but also as legal guardians for the MKs who lived with them. They would be responsible for us physically, emotionally and spiritually. They must attempt to be fair and firm in all their guidance and discipline. What a huge task they chose to accept!

The first ones to take on this immense responsibility were Uncle Flip and Aunt Esther Moneysmith. They were nearing retirement, however, by the time Tim, Tom and I came to live at Mid-Maples, so we were with them for only our freshman year.

Mid-Maples family with our next guardians, the Olsons, 1968
Larry is on the right in back; Tim, Tom, Dale are also in the picture

82

Then Uncle LaVerne and Aunt Beulah Olson took over as our guardians. I was especially happy to see the Olsons, because they had served as my dorm-parents at the MK elementary school in CAR, and Aunt Beulah was the one who, with the help of my sister Maribeth, led me years earlier to accept Jesus as my Savior.

What They Already Knew

Our first year at Mid-Maples, we attended a church in Lombard, Illinois. During our second year, the Olsons got us involved in a small church in nearby Winfield that needed some encouragement. But before long they decided we needed to be in a church where we would receive more guidance aimed specifically at the teens. So we began attending First Baptist Church of Medinah and stayed there through the rest of our high school years. I found it interesting that Pastor Don Hamman, the son of my former pastor in Indiana, was now my pastor at the Medinah church!

God continued to work in my life through Pastor Hamman's preaching, contributing to my spiritual growth. One Sunday evening after his message, when I was fourteen, I responded to the invitation and went forward. I felt that it was time to make public what God had been doing in my heart for years. God was calling me to be a missionary, and I wanted people to know it.

From the time of my earliest memories, I knew what my parents were doing as missionaries was important, and I wanted to be a missionary too. Further, I loved Africa, and sensed somehow that my future would involve this continent.

But, although I do not remember it, there *was* a time when I considered another occupation. I was three at the time. Our family had just arrived in the US for furlough. A newspaper reporter had come to our house to interview these unusual hometown folks who had given their lives to work as missionaries in the heart of Africa. I quote from her article of May 24, 1954, in the *South Bend Tribune* of South Bend, Indiana:

The children thrived on their life in the primitive land, and they look it. "But they are terribly excited right now about the trains and cars in America," Mrs. Fogle laughed. As

she said it little Larry, clambering over the reporter inter-
viewing his parents, shouted that he had just seen a "great
big train, with a man in it, too." It was explained to him that
a train must have a man to run it, so he decided immediately
that it would be his life's ambition to be an engineer.

Betraying my immediate interests I had blurted, "I'm going to drive a train when I grow up!"

Honestly, I don't remember ever wanting to be a train engineer. It was nothing more than a passing thought. I guess my childish mind was temporarily captured by this idea, as for the first time in my life I experienced the sights and sounds of a great big train lumbering down the track with its whistle blowing.

Anyway, the thought of becoming a train engineer didn't stick. What grew in my mind and heart through my childhood years was the desire to be a missionary. I made no secret of this!

Now fourteen years old, in church that Sunday evening, I sensed that God was leading me to make a public statement about my commitment to missions.

I would guess that most of the folks at my church were already aware of my intentions. So my public commitment that Sunday evening came as no surprise to them! I was only confirming what they already knew.

A Brand New High School

In previous years, the MKs staying at Mid-Maples all attended Wheaton Academy, but Wheaton North High School was closer to home. This was a brand new school, beginning with just 9th and 10th grade classes. They added a new class each year, so those in 10th grade in the school's first year became Wheaton North's first graduating class.

The three Fogle boys all started 9th grade together. Many people thought we were triplets. In the end, we were in Wheaton North's second graduating class.

I enjoyed high school at Wheaton North. I made friends, I got decent grades and I got involved in a number of activities.

But I was not successful at all the activities I tried. Baseball in 10th grade, for example! I did all right as an outfielder, I guess, but I was expecting the game to be a little more like softball. I never could get the hang of hitting that smaller baseball. *Why did they make the baseball so small?*

I Had Never Played Basketball Before

From my freshman year I decided that I wanted to play basketball. Although only 5'10" tall, I was lean, in pretty good shape and I could jump. The only problem was that I had never played basketball before. In fact, I had only seldom *held* a basketball before.

In try-outs for the freshman team, the coach must have thought he saw some potential in me. I say that because he certainly didn't see any *skill*! Anyway, I made the team. They kept twenty players on that freshman team, and I was number twenty. I was *waaaay* down on the end of the bench, and didn't see any game time all season.

I worked hard that summer, and improved a bit, and by my sophomore year I moved up to number fourteen. Of course they only kept fourteen players on the sophomore team . . . ! I did see two or three minutes of game time that season, and even scored my first points. Unfortunately, they were also my *only* points that season!

I chose not to play my junior year, but practiced hard all summer before my senior year and tried out for the varsity team. The coach had challenged us to shoot 10,000 baskets that summer – no, we were to *make* 10,000 baskets. I spent a lot of time on the basketball court in the Mid-Maples driveway that summer, and I made my 10,000 baskets – lay-ups, hooks, jump shots, longer set shots from all over the court, and left-handed shots of every variety too.

I didn't make the varsity team – it seems that the "I-think-he-has-some-potential" excuse for keeping me on the team was wearing thin by this time. But I will never regret accepting the coach's challenge. I became a far better player because of it, and learned a great deal about concentration and perseverance in the bargain.

The Duet Was Especially Traumatic

Music was a big thing for me in high school. From the first year, I got involved in the fledgling chorus, and later became part of the men's glee club, madrigal ensemble and barbershop quartet. Then came my senior year. In the school's spring musical, I sang a solo, "Some Enchanted Evening," and a duet, "Younger than Springtime." My performance was not stellar. Let's just say it wasn't the beginning of an illustrious career on the stage.

Larry as a high-school senior, 1968

The duet was especially traumatic. It was to be a romantic duet, sung from the heart to my "sweetheart." I was cast with a sweet girl with a sweet voice. Looking into each other's eyes at the end of the song, we were to hold hands and blend our voices in heavenly harmony toward a rich, musical climax. Then, as the echoes of those notes died away, and before the thunderous applause began, I was to clasp my girl in a "never-let-her-go" embrace and give her a kiss she would never forget.

That isn't how it happened.

When the school's music director told me I would be singing this duet with this girl, I was excited to have been chosen. I was even okay with holding her hands and looking into her eyes. But kiss her? *Kiss her? Full on the lips?* I had never ever kissed a girl before, and I wasn't about to give my first kiss in full sight of hundreds of people at a public event! *There is no way this is going to happen* . . . . I think I lamely mumbled something about not believing in kissing someone I wasn't going to marry.

So we sang the song. I held the hands of my "sweetheart" and looked into her eyes. We arrived at the climactic moment at the end of the song. As the final notes hung in the air, and as the applause began, I quickly dropped the girl's hands and rushed off stage, leaving her to find her own way.

So much for my budding reputation as a suave and polished "ladies' man."

In Time for Our Graduation

Dad and Mom returned from Africa in time for our graduation. They *had* to be there for this graduation – they had three boys graduating from the same school on the same day!

Three guys with the same last name . . . about the same size . . . in the same grade.

It happened that I graduated before my older twin brothers. Not long before – just seconds. Alphabetically, my name was called before theirs, so I took my turn before they did.

"Larry Luke Fogle." I crossed the platform, received my diploma, and shook the principal's hand.

"Thomas John Fogle." You could hear the whispering across the auditorium: *They must be twins* . . . . *I heard there were some twins in the class.* Tom received his diploma.

"Timothy James Fogle." Now there was widespread chatter: *Not only twins – they must be triplets!* After Tim had received his diploma and left the platform, the principal had to wait until the noise died away before the name of the next graduate could be read.

At our graduation, I had the privilege of directing a senior choir composed of about eighty of my classmates. Particularly appropriate was one song we performed: "Climb every mountain; ford every stream; follow every rainbow, till you find your dream."

Mom, Tim, Tom, Larry, Dale at high school graduation, 1968

We were proud to have our long-absent parents present. Here was certain proof of their love for us – if our long-term separation from them had ever caused us to doubt. Our parents had left Africa and come back to the US in time for our graduation! All was well with the world.

8

ON MY OWN THROUGH COLLEGE: 1968 – 1973

An Intriguing "Coincidence"

Convinced that God's plan for me gave my life eternal significance, I was very serious about my approach to college.

Where would I go to college? During my last couple of years in high school, I investigated the options. Above all, because God had called me to be a missionary, I wanted an education in Bible and Missions.

To properly train for my future ministry, I would not consider a school that did not offer me these essentials.

Several Bible schools were carefully considered. Each offered a Bible major and a Missions minor. But I took a special look at a school in Grand Rapids, Michigan, which at that time was known as Grand Rapids Baptist Bible College (GRBBC).

Dr. Paul Beals, a former BMM missionary in central Africa, had for years led the Missions Department of the Grand Rapids school with distinction. I was delighted that I could receive my Missions training from a missionary statesman and professor of Missions who had such an excellent reputation. On top of that, he was someone I already knew and respected!

Then I discovered that the school had just begun to offer a minor in Linguistics, the study of the structure and features of language. Dr. Henry Osborn, a former BMM missionary and Bible translator in Venezuela, and a noted linguist, was responsible for the development of the new Linguistics program. What a privilege it would be to study under one who was so highly respected in his field!

Languages had always interested me. In fact, when I had formally given my life to God for missions at the age of fourteen, I thought His call might involve Bible translation. So when I found out that GRBBC now offered a Linguistics minor, I was intrigued by this "coincidence."

The Bible and missions programs I needed were already in place. The added attraction of a Linguistics minor made my decision to attend GRBBC an easy one. The scholarship they offered me just sweetened the deal!

On My Own – with God

My missionary parents were home on furlough during my first year in college. They supported my decision to attend Grand Rapids Baptist Bible College, and in a number of ways were a great encouragement to me that year. However, they weren't in a position to help with my college expenses. I was on my own financially.

There is no reason why I should have expected my parents to help with the expenses of my college years.

GRBBC costs at that time were fairly minimal anyway – if I remember right, tuition plus room and board totaled only about $1,000 per semester!

But the seven kids in our family knew that our parents' missionary support was not sufficient to allow them to help us financially as we went off to college. Dad and Mom had not been able to help with college expenses for Lois, Phil or Maribeth. Why would I think they would be able to help *me*?

The possibility of my parents' financial help would have seemed all the more remote when one remembered that there were three of us starting college in the same year!

Instead of being envious of certain other students whose parents were in a position to help *them* financially, I saw this as a special opportunity to learn to trust God to provide for me.

Years Crucial to My Development

My purpose for going to college was well-defined: these would be years of preparation for a lifetime of ministry. I was motivated. I was determined. I was eager to learn. I was ready to discipline myself. I wanted to become all I could be.

The five years I spent in Bible college were formative years for me, years that were crucial to my development. This time period – with the decisions and disciplines and lessons it brought into my life – was absolutely foundational for the person I was to become.

My studies were important to me. I had some great roommates during my years in college, but especially valuable to me was a roommate my first two years. Like me, George was aiming for ministry and, on top of that, was a serious student. We competed for top grades, but we were also supportive of each other. We often studied together into the early morning hours, each of us seeking to encourage the other when energy and motivation began to lag.

George and I often kept ourselves going late at night by eating popcorn as we studied. I'm afraid the other guys in the dorm often suffered with the tantalizing smell of our fresh-popped treat. One school year, we went through a total of forty-two *pounds* of popcorn!

The study habits, the determination and the self-discipline I learned in those first two years set the pattern for the rest of my college years – and, indeed, for the rest of my life.

I never could understand how others in the dorm could fritter away their evening hours – spending hours in front of the television, playing Rook, or wandering the halls visiting friends – all the while complaining loudly to others about the heavy load of homework assigned by the professors! Of course, these were often the same students who offered excuses why they had not been able to complete an assignment, or who puzzled over why they had gotten a "D" or "F" grade for a test when others received an "A" or "B."

As I observed these undisciplined students, then paused to consider myself, I came to understand an important life lesson: *Who we will be tomorrow is determined by who we allow ourselves to be today.* A lazy, careless or sloppy young person is building into his life habits that will, to some extent, define him for a lifetime. Apart from God's kind intervention, these same traits may severely limit his potential for using his life to achieve anything significant.

You Can Be Serious and Have Fun Too!

Studies didn't occupy all my time at college! Being serious about my studies didn't mean I had to reconcile myself to "no fun" through college. Being focused on ministry preparation didn't mean I couldn't enjoy a variety of wholesome activities. In fact, I think I enjoyed college life *more* because, after fulfilling my study responsibilities, I could set my studies aside in good conscience. Without feeling guilty, I could now fully enjoy the various experiences of an active college life.

I managed to carve out time one year to play varsity soccer, alternating between the halfback and fullback positions. Another year I joined the varsity track team – running the 440, the 880 and various relays.

Basketball was a sport I really enjoyed. The intramural basketball league attracted my attention for at least two years. It was satisfying to end up as second highest scorer one season. Some suggested that I should be playing varsity basketball, but I knew I wasn't able to compete on that level.

In the end, I didn't allow myself to focus too much time and energy on sports. The level of commitment required in order to master the sport – the time and effort it would demand to keep up with regular team training, for example – would, I felt, inevitably detract from the focus God wanted me to place on studies and ministry experience.

There was, however, *always* time for dating! I liked the girls as much as the next guy. There were so many wonderful Christian girls at this Bible college – and I dated quite a few of them. Some of them would have made fine missionary wives. But God had someone special waiting for me, someone I would not even meet until a year after I *left* Bible college. How thankful I am that God saved us for each other!

There were concerts, there were ball games, there were banquets and there were parties. Oh yes, the parties . . .

Although serious and focused, I was also known to be outgoing, enthusiastic and fun-loving. In my early days at college, I was pulled into a couple of short skits, and before long people were calling on me to organize and produce the skits for various parties and other college functions.

On one memorable occasion, this "skit man" was asked to provide thirty minutes of entertainment for the school-wide Valentine Banquet. I loved the challenge and excitement of doing an event like that but, of course, it could only be done with the help and cooperation of a number of other student comedians.

At another school event, in the presence of both faculty and students, a number of carefully-chosen students performed intricately-planned routines, mimicking the eccentric habits and characteristics of certain popular professors. We didn't even have to announce the names of the ones we were mimicking; it was immediately evident to the crowd. But this was all done in good fun. Even the professors at whom we were poking fun found the good-natured mimicry hilarious – in fact, they seemed to laugh the loudest!

The Big One with the Pony Tail

God had given me a special interest in music, and a real desire to use my minimal abilities for His glory.

The college chorale was something for which I would make time! I considered it a real privilege to be a part of this forty-voice choir for four years. Under the capable direction of Rev. Desmond Bell, this choir developed a full, rich sound that seemed to me to be quite professional. We appreciated Rev. Bell's insistence on excellence, his gentlemanly leadership and his godly example. His wife usually joined us on our scheduled concert outings on weekends and during our yearly concert tour during spring break. She provided a sweet, motherly presence among this gang of college students.

I remember one ten-day concert tour which took us south and east from Michigan. As president of the chorale that year, I was determined to make our tour an occasion for evangelistic outreach as we traveled through Michigan, Ohio, West Virginia, Virginia and North Carolina. In general, I wanted the tour to be a growing experience, a spiritual highlight for our musicians.

The chorale members accepted my challenge to pray for and seek out opportunities to witness in our travels and in our meetings. When our chartered bus stopped along the way to allow us to eat a meal or use the restroom, our students passed out tracts and witnessed to individuals God led across their paths. It was often difficult to get our people back onto the bus so that we could arrive at our next destination on time! Several people made the decision to believe in Jesus during these brief stops.

Our concerts themselves provided more opportunities for personal evangelism. We presented concerts in churches every night of the week and twice on Sunday. We began to actively seek out specific individuals among those attending these concerts, approaching them to ask them about their personal faith in Jesus Christ.

One concert took place in Rocky Mount, North Carolina. During the first half of our concert, God drew our attention to a group of four young men seated in the back row.

This bunch of guys was in church, but they looked like they weren't happy to be there. Their shoulder-length hair and casual dress were not commonly accepted in churches in those years. They took courage from each other by hanging together, sitting together in the back row.

It was clear that these guys valued their independence. They wanted to be themselves, to develop their own identities. I could understand that. I had always found it curious, however, that such people would refuse to fit in with a certain group of people (in the church, for example), only to end up imitating *other* people. In reality, these four guys in North Carolina were no closer to establishing their own identities. Instead of developing personal, internal qualities that would distinguish them, they were all about copying external characteristics: they dressed like each other, they wore their hair like each other and they sat with each other as far back in the church as they could. They even imitated each other in the way they sat, slouching and crossing their arms.

From the platform, most of the choir members had noticed these four young men in the back. During our mid-concert break, we made some assignments. "Jon, after the concert you talk to the skinny guy on the aisle. Dave, you take the red-haired guy next to him. Jim, the guy with the glasses and moustache is yours. And the tough guy on the right, the big one with the pony tail . . . "

"*You* take him, Larry! *You* talk to him." Oh, no! He was the one I was most afraid to confront! So I began to prepare my heart to share the Gospel with this "tough guy."

Other choir members identified additional people in the congregation whom God had laid on their hearts. We prayed together, asking for God's blessing not only on the remaining portion of our concert but also on our evangelistic efforts at the end of the service.

During the closing prayer, a number of us left the platform and quietly made our way to the foyer of the church. As soon as the "Amen" was said, the four guys tried to make a quick exit, but we were there waiting for them. I approached the big one with the pony tail, looked him right in the eye and asked him if he had ever made that all-important decision to trust Jesus Christ for his salvation.

He was a bit flustered as he responded, "No, I guess I haven't really done that."

"Would you be willing to let me talk to you alone, so you can go home tonight with your sins forgiven and with peace in your heart?"

Agreeing, this big tough guy followed me without argument into the nearby church nursery, where we perched precariously on toddler-size chairs. He could not have been more compliant. He didn't interrupt me at all while I laid out God's simple plan of salvation. He was so ready to hear this!

At the end of my presentation, I asked him if he was ready to receive Jesus as his Savior. I didn't even need to urge him to bow his head. In his simple and tearful prayer, he confessed his sinfulness, thanked God for sending Jesus to earth to die for his sin and asked Jesus to be his Savior.

Through the ministry of our choir members, six people trusted Christ at the church that evening. All in all, during that ten-day choir tour, sixteen people were saved! The choir returned to school with such excitement about how God had used us!

What a lesson we had learned about God's work in bringing a person to salvation. We should never assume by a person's looks or actions that he is too hard-hearted to believe. We should never doubt God's ability to prepare that person's heart for our witness. We had also learned a lesson about what God is willing to do through us if we are willing to step out in faith, under His guidance, to confront people with the Gospel!

It Wasn't Just a Tool

There were two summers between my college years when I was not touring with a gospel quartet. I needed a job those two summers which would allow me to earn some money toward my college bills. One of those summers I accepted the invitation to go home with a college friend, Kevin Thomas, to Erie, Pennsylvania, where I could work through the summer.

The other summer I returned home to northern Indiana, where I got a job with my twin brothers, Tim and Tom, at a mobile home factory in Elkhart. It was a huge place, containing a number of departments where specific parts of the mobile home were built before passing the unit along for the next stage of assembly.

The three of us usually worked together some distance down the line. Our assignment was to position the long side walls of the mobile home on either side of us as they were swung over to us on pulleys, and work our way down between the walls. As we went, we were to unroll fiberglass insulation vertically between the two-by-four wall "studs" and staple narrow wood straps horizontally across the studs to hold the insulation in place.

All this was to be done efficiently, before the side walls could be moved along the line to be attached to the floor of the mobile home – which by this time had the plumbing and flooring all in place.

The tools we used to do our work were a common "box-knife," used to cut the roll of fiberglass insulation at the proper length when fitting it between the wall studs, and a large, heavy-duty, compressed-air staple gun, used to staple the wood straps which held the insulation in place. All you had to do was to press the head of the staple gun against the wood, and with a sharp *phoot!* the two-inch staple would be driven deep into the wood. You could move very quickly down the line – *phoot! phoot! phoot! phoot!* – and that wood strap would be secure.

One day, Tom and I were fitting the insulation while Tim was working with the staple gun. All three of us were maneuvering within the narrow alley between the two side walls, stepping around rolls of insulation and a bundle of wood straps, and trying to avoid getting entangled in the long snake-like compressed-air hose for the staple gun.

I was moving along from one end of a side wall, while Tim – *phoot! phoot!* – worked in my direction from the opposite end of the other side wall. Preoccupied with my task, I was surprised when Tim backed into me with the large staple gun dangling from his hand. *Phoot!* As the head of the staple gun pressed against my hip, a two-inch staple was automatically discharged and driven deep into my hip.

On the job, I always carried a heavy, wadded-up bandanna in my left hip pocket. I pulled it out every few minutes throughout the hot day, to wipe the perspiration from my face and neck. Well, I couldn't have pulled it out now! The heavy-duty staple had penetrated the layers of my clothing, wadded-up bandanna and all, and pinned it deep into my left hip socket.

It seems that staple gun was more than a tool – it was also a weapon!

After evaluating the situation, my brothers accompanied me as I hobbled in a stiff-legged gait up to the front office, not wanting to agitate the affected hip socket. An ambulance was called, and before long I found myself in the emergency room of the local hospital. Medical staff cut my clothes off around the staple and tried to determine how to deal with the situation. It seems they couldn't decide whether I needed a doctor or a carpenter to take care of the problem!

In the end, several nurses stood on one side of me holding me on the table, while a doctor stood on the other side of the table and used a hefty pair of pliers to try to yank the staple out. After several failed attempts, which threatened to wrestle me off the table and onto the floor, one final heroic jerk pulled the staple free! I was soon on my way home.

As for Tim, I did notice that for the rest of the summer he stayed clear of me on the job whenever I had the staple gun in *my* hand! That was, perhaps, the better part of wisdom.

Learning to Serve

During my college years I sang with two different gospel quartets. For almost two years, I sang with a quartet called the *Conquerors*, then another year with another quartet by the same name.

Larry with the first Conquerors *quartet, 1970*
Left to right: David Slagg, Dick Winne, Dennis Weiler, Don Zwyghuizen, Larry

Both of these male quartets left me with great memories of warm friendship, hilarious fun and tremendous ministry experience.

Each quartet traveled on weekends throughout the school year, representing the school in church ministries and youth meetings of various kinds. These weekend ministries were exhausting as we usually had to return to school Sunday evening after our church service. Returning from our trips, we hardly ever got to bed before midnight and sometimes not until 3 or 4 in the morning. Then of course we had to be ready for our classes when, just a few hours later, the new day of school began! Or when occasionally we returned on Monday from longer out-of-state trips, we always had to play catch-up with our classes.

A ten-week summer tour with one quartet took us through Michigan, Ohio, West Virginia, Pennsylvania and New York. A similar opportunity with the other quartet another summer took us through Michigan, Indiana, Illinois, Wisconsin, Minnesota and Iowa. Again we were involved in Sunday church services, mid-week concerts, teen rallies and youth meetings of various kinds.

In addition, we did four or five weeks of summer youth camps – counseling in the boys' cabins, providing special music all during the week and interacting with the youth at every level for their spiritual benefit. We took these responsibilities very seriously, and God used us to encourage many young people to passionately follow Christ.

Traveling with these quartets provided me invaluable experience. I learned important lessons about such things as interpersonal relationships, faithfulness and dependability, confidence in front of people, communication, self-discipline and time management.

I have never wished to go back to those earlier years, because through our lives God has taken us on from one great adventure to another. But I have sometimes paused to remember with fondness the intense ministry, the close camaraderie and the great fun of those days, as we grew in the Lord and learned to serve.

The Heavy Burden of Leadership

God permitted me to learn to serve in another way during my last year in college – as "Resident Advisor" in Quincer Hall, the dormitory for men in their first year at the college.

Each year, upperclassmen were appointed to serve in the dorms among the new students. For the ninety freshmen in Quincer Hall, one Resident Advisor was entrusted with their leadership. Three other upperclassmen were appointed as Resident Assistants, who would work alongside the Resident Advisor. The four were strategically placed through the dorm, as their job was to orient, guide and counsel the freshmen. The RAs (as they were called) were always careful to select roommates who would be exemplary and supportive of their ministry among the students.

With two years left before graduation, I was given the opportunity to move back into the freshman dorm to room with the newly-appointed Resident Advisor for the dorm. Then for my last year in college, that appointment fell in my direction.

By this time, I had served in a number of leadership capacities on campus. But my experience the previous year had taught me something about the immensity of this particular responsibility. Now I would be faced with the heavy weight of that very responsibility.

God led me to accept the challenge. Looking back, I can see that God was stretching me and maturing me in new ways that year, to prepare me for other leadership responsibilities later in my life. Together with my team we faced issues among the students such as poor study habits, poor time management, confusion about God's will, rebellion against authority, thievery, gross immorality, anger leading to violence, severe depression and even what appeared to be demon possession.

By the end of that year, I had discovered how little I knew about being a good leader. In fact, I had discovered that it is much easier *not to be* the leader! The challenges, the interruptions, the expectations, the long hours, the lack of appreciation, the criticisms, the burdens you bear for those under your leadership, the sense of failure you sometimes feel as your best efforts do not achieve the results for which you had hoped . . . Wow, the load of leadership is a heavy one to carry!

I Wanted to Be Sure

During that last year of college, I was carrying another heavy burden. *Only one more year of school before I can go back to Africa as a missionary*, I promised myself in great anticipation. *But wait a minute! Is this something I want to do because Africa still seems like home to me, or is it really what God wants me to do? Is this my will or is it God's will?*

It was clear to me that a Christian will be miserable if he finds himself outside the will of God. I did not want to make a mistake about such an important matter! I wanted to be sure.

This began a year-long process of seeking to know for sure what God wanted me to do. I cleared my mind of my own agenda, and began to earnestly seek God's will with an "open mind." I spent more time with God in Bible study and focused prayer. I told God I wanted to give Him a fair opportunity to change the direction of my life if He did not want me to be a missionary.

Aware of how significant godly counsel can be when seeking to know God's will, I sought out a number of godly leaders whose counsel I knew I could trust. These leaders reassured me with their unanimous counsel. "God has given you the ideal background and training to make missionary service a natural option for you to consider. On top of that, He has given you a love for missionary work and a love for Africa. That is God's doing. It seems obvious to us, and to everybody else around you, that God has called you to be a missionary."

Largely through the counsel I received from these men, I came to understand better how God works. From a practical standpoint, God often leads a believer to know what He wants him to do with his life by placing in his heart a strong desire to do something. This is a holy desire that focuses him on doing something significant for the glory of God. It is an increasing desire that grows stronger and stronger over time. It is an unshakable desire that won't go away.

That's the way it was for me.

My passionate quest for an undeniable conviction about God's will for my life continued for a year. Over time, I had to acknowledge that I could not envision my future apart from missionary service. God had so focused me on serving Him as a missionary, with such an increasing and unshakable desire, that I could no longer deny God's will for my life.

I had asked God to lead me. He had done that. Now it was time to get moving.

Great Preparation for Missions

Some people have asked, "In my education, what is the best way to prepare for missions?" Clearly, God doesn't lead everybody in the same way. In some cases, a person is not even called to be a missionary until after receiving a secular university education, or even after working for years in a secular job. But in other cases, a person senses God's leading into missions early in life and can plan his education strategically toward that end. I would recommend to that person that he pursue a Bible major and a Missions minor, along with another minor and the kind of electives that will be useful to him as a missionary.

In my case, the Bible major and the Missions minor I received were just what I needed. But in Michigan the requirements were clear: a Bible major could be granted only with two "secular" minors, and missions did not qualify. I was therefore required to have two other minors in addition to my minor in missions. Linguistics and a (combined) Speech/English focus served as my two secular minors.

The problem was that you can't fit a major and *three* minors into a normal four-year college program. So I chose to spend a fifth year in college. That allowed me to complete my third minor, thereby fulfilling the requirements for graduation. I would not graduate with the same class with which I started college, but that didn't bother me.

This fifth year also allowed me to begin my seminary studies. Of course, this required special permission, because I would be taking seminary classes while I was still completing my college classes!

When I graduated at the end of that fifth year, my missionary parents were still overseas. Understanding the situation, Dr. and Mrs. John Balyo offered to stand in as my "parents" at my graduation. I really appreciated their kindness because nobody from my family was able to be there to share this special occasion with me.

Looking back, I am so thankful for the way God led me, to give me just the right kind of preparation to serve me well throughout our missionary career.

9

EXCITING DAYS: 1973 – 1974

I Still Had a Lot to Learn!

Having finally reached that seemingly elusive goal of graduation, I faced the great temptation which faces everybody who
reaches such a major milestone in his life. "You have learned so
much . . . . You're ready now. Go do what you want to do! Get out
there and make your mark on the world!"

The problem is not in the accomplished goal – that's a wonderful thing! The problem is not in the eager ambition of the young
graduate, nor in the fresh potential of his life.

Instead, the problem is in the know-it-all attitude that says, "The
world has been waiting for all I have to offer. Here I am, world!
Look out, here I come!" It is assumed that book knowledge is more
important than the know-how, wisdom and discernment that come
with age and experience. "Move over, veterans, I'm here now. I'll
show you how to do it!"

As I stepped out to take my place in the world, I shared all the
eagerness and zeal of the average graduate. These were exciting
days!

Yet I had to remind myself that my academic learning could
not compensate for my lack of experience – in fact, I still had a lot
to learn! Instead of being ready to take over, I needed to humble
myself to learn *real-life ministry* from those who could mentor me
and serve as ministry models for me.

They Tried to Tempt Me to Stay

My next goal had been to return to Africa as a missionary as soon as I was done with my schooling. I had not envisioned that God wanted me to get some ministry experience in the local church before he would let me go.

To stay alive, I needed to have some income while I worked on filling out the extensive questionnaire and doctrinal papers for Baptist Mid-Missions.

Right out of college, I returned to northern Indiana and took a temporary job delivering furniture for a quality furniture store in Elkhart. My bosses knew that I would not be staying long. I made no secret of the fact that my life belonged to the Lord Jesus Christ, and before long I would leave their employment to serve God as a missionary in Africa. They couldn't comprehend that kind of thinking.

I could have been content delivering furniture if that's what God had called me to do. But that wasn't where my heart was. When the opportunity arose for me to get some ministry experience by serving in a church, I approached my bosses with my resignation. They tried to tempt me to stay, offering me a raise and a promotion in position. All I could say was, "I appreciate your offer and your confidence in me but, honestly, what you are offering to me doesn't even interest me. I know what God wants me to do . . . . And it's what *I* want to do!"

Valuable Experience in the Local Church

Immanuel Baptist Church in Annandale, Virginia, extended me an invitation to serve them as their Youth Pastor. But we had an understanding. The church had already called a man to be their Assistant Pastor, whose duties were to include working with the youth, so they needed my help for only a short time. It was a perfect arrangement; I could help them for only a short time. I ministered there about eight months.

It was a great privilege to work side by side with a godly, experienced pastor, Pastor Ollie Goad, who had a reputation for integrity and dignity in the ministry. What a blessing it was for this exuberant novice that such a man would welcome him as a colleague and mentor him in ministry.

My paperwork for Baptist Mid-Missions was still in process, and God had other lessons for me to learn. So I accepted another temporary ministry assignment, this time working with youth and music in a smaller church in a much smaller town – First Baptist Church of Ithaca, Michigan. Again an experienced pastor took me under his wing and allowed me to learn under his leadership. This church, like the other one, knew ahead of time of my desire to soon be in Africa.

I valued the four months I spent in Ithaca, for Pastor Charles Steiner gave me opportunity to get involved in various facets of the ministry, including one-on-one discipleship with new believers which helped to feed my life-long passion for discipleship. He also let me see the "inside" of church ministry in a way which helped me understand the realities of life as a pastor.

What I learned through those local-church experiences in those short months later proved to be of inestimable value in my own missionary ministries among national pastors. All the more so because before this I had had little consistent involvement with any one local church!

As the young child of missionary parents I was always visiting different churches with Dad and Mom – both in their itinerant ministry among African churches and as they reported to their supporting churches in the US. Oh, we had a home church, but we could not be there on a consistent basis. That was the reality of our lives.

Then as a teenager living in the MK boarding home in Illinois, I attended church regularly with the other MKs, but partway through my high-school years, our guardians determined that we should transfer from the church we were attending to another. A wise move for our spiritual development? Undoubtedly! But we did not have the opportunity to develop a long-term commitment to one church. Our relationship with one church was curtailed and our relationship with the other was destined to be short.

Finally, in five years of college and seminary in Michigan, I was constantly moving about from one church to another. Singing with two gospel quartets and the college chorale, I traveled most weekends during the school year to represent the school. Occasionally, I would use a free Sunday to drive two and a half hours to visit my older sister in northern Indiana. So rarely did I find myself at the college on a Sunday, I didn't develop a loyalty to any one church during those five years! Instead, on those rare occasions when I *was* in town, I tended to visit various churches depending on where an outstanding preacher would be speaking that day, or where a special concert would be presented – or even where a certain girl would be attending!

Now, with that background . . . God knew what He was doing when He led me to spend some concentrated time, even if minimal, under a pastor's mentorship in a local church. I am so thankful that God did not allow me to return to Africa until I gained that little bit of ministry experience within the local church.

A Cantata Like That . . . A Pie Like That

Two events come to mind from my brief ministry in Ithaca, Michigan.

The coming of spring led to the first of these two memorable events. Thinking ahead to Easter, I began to dream about leading a musical cantata – my first ever – for the encouragement of this small-town church.

Okay, how do you produce a quality musical cantata when you have only a small congregation and only a few musicians among them? Puzzling over the problem, only two solutions presented themselves. We could work with a larger group of aspiring singers – but time was very short and I knew it would be difficult to prepare something of quality if those with less musical ability were included. The other choice was to use a smaller group of more capable musicians, and work toward an excellent musical presentation.

But who has ever heard of an Easter cantata performed by a small group? Well . . . , was there any good reason why we couldn't try it?

We ended up with a twelve-voice ensemble. Each person dedicated himself to serious practice, and the cantata started to come together. We promoted the special event with enthusiasm.

On Easter Sunday evening, people entering the church auditorium received a printed program and were escorted to their seats. The house lights were dimmed and the colored spotlights borrowed from the local high school lit up the platform as the cantata began. The program flowed smoothly, the harmony was rich and the message was heart-felt and clear. It turned out to be an inspiring evening – and a highlight of my time in Ithaca.

The second memory that comes to mind from my time in Ithaca was a comic event that demonstrated Pastor Steiner's quick wit.

One Sunday, an older lady in the congregation presented him a fruit pie she had baked fresh just that morning. She was delighted to know that her pastor's family would enjoy *her pie* as dessert for their Sunday dinner.

Still single at the time, I had a room in the basement of the pastor's home, and I ate my meals with his family. So I knew I would get my share of that pie!

That Sunday we enjoyed a delicious dinner, and finally it was time for the lady's mouth-watering pie. Our first bites, however, made us gag – something was desperately wrong with this pie! This lady had a reputation for baking wonderful pies, but somehow . . . she had made a serious mistake with the recipe this time. There was nothing to do but to throw the pie down the garbage disposal.

Now we had a problem. What would we say to the kind lady at the evening service? She was bound to ask, "How did you like the pie?"

Sure enough, even before the evening service began, the well-meaning cook approached pastor with her question: "Did you all enjoy the pie?" Pastor did not want to lie, but neither did he want to hurt the dear lady's feelings. His response came out something like this, "Knowing your reputation as a cook, ma'am, we could hardly wait through dinner to get to dessert. And, wow . . . All I can say is . . . *A pie like that doesn't last long around our house!*"

Finally, Back to Africa!

With my doctrinal statement for Baptist Mid-Missions still in progress, I remained a step short of full-time missionary status. Since I was still single and able to move around without encumbrance, BMM approached me about returning to the Central African Republic as a short-termer to help with some immediate needs on the field. My parents had been on furlough during the previous year, and were now preparing to return to CAR. So I could return with them.

"Since you are focused on CAR anyway, why don't you go back with your parents now as a short-termer? You already know the language, so you could help immediately by teaching in the Bible School and speaking among the African churches. Continue to work on your doctrinal statement while you are there. When you are ready, you can return to the US to face the BMM General Council for your doctrinal examination and full authorization. Then you will be able to proceed with deputation to raise your support for full-time missionary service."

Well, all this made perfect sense to a young, single man who was eager to get back to Africa! Eleven years had passed since I had last seen Africa, and my heart was still there.

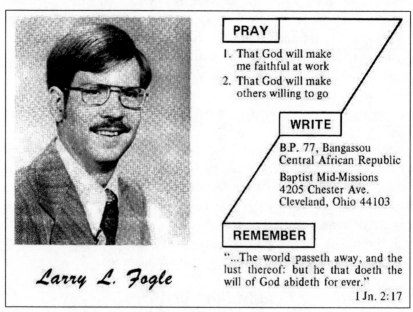

PRAY

1. That God will make me faithful at work
2. That God will make others willing to go

WRITE

B.P. 77, Bangassou
Central African Republic

Baptist Mid-Missions
4205 Chester Ave.
Cleveland, Ohio 44103

REMEMBER

"...The world passeth away, and the lust thereof: but he that doeth the will of God abideth for ever."

I Jn. 2:17

Larry L. Fogle

Prayer card for short term in CAR, 1974-1975

Before I could leave, however, there were several realities I needed to face.

First, even as a short-termer, I needed a little bit of financial support to cover my trip and my expenses in CAR. While serving at the

Ithaca church that spring and during the early summer, God gave me the opportunity to present my ministry in several churches. God provided about $250 in monthly support plus special gifts to cover my ticket to the field.

Second, BMM wanted me to attend their Candidate Seminar that summer before leaving. This would not ordinarily be expected for a short-termer, but in light of the fact that I was in the process of my application for full-time service, it seemed wise for me to have that orientation before establishing myself on the CAR field.

Third, I had to face the reality that, during my time in Africa as a single man, I could not entertain any hope of developing a guy-girl relationship that could lead toward marriage. There was at the time no prospect in view and . . . *what prospects could I expect to meet while in Africa?* After all, the Christian girls that I knew about in CAR were either single missionary ladies – I have nothing against single missionary ladies, but these were all middle-aged or older and I was only 24! – or African girls of a vastly different culture. No, I was going to have to forget about girls for the next year. For a healthy young male, this was a far bigger issue than you might think.

Finally, these hurdles were behind me. Finally, back to Africa!

Larry at airport with parents on way to CAR, August 1974

Arriving at the mission station, my parents and I were dropped off with our luggage where we would be staying, with instructions to put our things inside and wash up quickly. Supper was ready.

All the guests were to eat that evening with a missionary couple who were "Dad and Mom" not only to their own offspring, but also to a few other high-school-aged MKs. These teens were in Bangui to attend the small MK high school located there on the mission property, a high school option that had become available since I left central Africa in 1963.

Walking into our hosts' dining room, we found that most people, missionaries and MKs alike, had already taken their seats at the table. Across the room I noticed an attractive, red-haired girl who carried herself very well. My parents had preceded me into the room and took their places, leaving two seats side by side. Uh . . . I was a bit flustered by this unexpected turn of events.

As Sallie and I took those two remaining seats at the table, I thought to myself, *My, my! What do we have* here? And I was lost, irretrievably lost.

Girls were back, full force, in the forefront of my thoughts again. *Oh, where is my self-discipline?* All intentions of putting girls out of my mind during my time in Africa were gone! No, I should correct that. My thoughts were all focused on one *particular* girl!

Sallie Tells Her Side of the Story

When many missionaries give their testimonies, they begin by stating their claim as an MK, a PK (preacher's kid) or even a DK (deacon's kid). I often begin by stating that I am an NK. Not being raised in the family of a missionary, a pastor or a deacon, I was a "Normal Kid." My mother and grandmother were godly women. I was born in Michigan but moved to Long Island, New York, where I attended public school.

I was saved at a young age in Vacation Bible School at my grandma's church, and enjoyed the years I spent in Pioneer Girls' club and church youth group. I was intrigued with missions, missionaries and foreign countries. My mom remembers my stated goals of traveling the world and having a maid.

I had a strong desire to seek and follow God's will for my life. I am thankful for a pastor who encouraged me. After high school graduation I found myself in the Chicago area, attending West Suburban Hospital School of Nursing. Associated with Wheaton College, the school had a wonderful influence on my growth as a Christian as well as in many other areas.

Sallie takes a break from studying at West Sub, 1974

One of the programs they encouraged was a summer missionary internship overseas. Through the guidance of my pastor in New York, I applied to Baptist Mid-Missions to do an internship with them the summer between my junior and senior years.

On my application to BMM I wrote that I was interested in going to Australia or England (thinking of being able to communicate) but NOT AFRICA. I was soon accepted into the program – but the only place they had for a nursing student was in *Bangassou*, Central African Republic. With much trepidation I agreed and began preparations for going.

That was the summer of 1974. My father worked for Pan American Airways at the time; using his employee discount my parents accompanied me as far as Paris. As this was also their first time overseas, we spent a couple days finding our way around Paris before I continued on to Africa by myself.

My ticket took me through the capital city *Bangui* all the way to *Bangassou* in eastern CAR. This was a mystery to all the missionaries, for there had never been any dependable scheduled flights to that far end of the earth. But there was a rare scheduled flight that week and I had a reservation to be on it.

However if the diplomat going on that rare flight finds it inconvenient to travel that day, then everyone politely waits to leave the following day. That is exactly what happened.

Since there was no way to communicate any change of plans to the missionaries in *Bangassou*, they had learned to play it by ear, listening for the plane to arrive. When my plane did arrive at the small dirt airstrip with its simple shack there was no one to meet me.

Knowing I could not speak French or the common "trade" language *Sango*, the missionaries had left a note for me that was delivered by a child. I was instructed to stay there with my baggage and wait. They would hear the plane fly over and soon come to get me. "Soon" can seem like a long time when everyone else leaves the airstrip and you have no way of communicating. They did come before long and I was whisked away to the mission station.

During my six-week stay I lived with and worked mainly with missionary nurse Ruth Nephew. I could help in Ruth's home by cleaning and cooking and in the dispensary also by cleaning and sorting old medicines. I could observe her medical work and children's classes, but communication was a problem and I was homesick and frustrated.

By the time Ruth and I left to travel by truck back to the capital city, I was able to tell God that I would return to CAR if that was His will. But I did not see how I could live the single missionary life as Ruth did. We visited the mission hospital at *Ippy* on our way to *Bangui* where I would catch my flight home.

At Bangassou *Sallie visits the grave of William Haas,*
founder of BMM, summer 1974

During the time I had been at *Bangassou* many of the Africans had asked Ruth if I was a Fogle. My red hair immediately placed me in that family in their eyes. I had never known or met the Fogles.

The missionaries were sorry I was leaving so quickly as the Fogles were soon returning to *Bangassou* and their college-graduate son was coming with them to work for a while. I was not interested at all, especially since I was not enjoying Africa.

Larry described our first meeting quite well. The missionaries and the high school students in *Bangui* all had the same thing in mind. They often placed us together during those few days, but there was no place to be off by ourselves. Larry did surprise me by accompanying those who took me to the airport and even gave me a kiss as I left.

When I returned home and told my family about my summer, my mother asked if I was going to write to this young man. I did not think I would, but when she said that this would be a kind thing to do, the letter writing began.

The Agony of a Long-Distance Courtship

This is Larry again. Settling into my parents' simple brick home at *Bangassou*, I became fully immersed in my missionary work, teaching in the Bible School located on the mission property and speaking among the African churches in the *Bangassou* area.

Sallie was never far from my thoughts. I did not wait long to write to her.

However, I knew it might be six weeks before Sallie would receive my letter. Then, assuming she answered right away, it might be another six weeks before I would receive her response. I was elated when I got her first letter before the expected three months passed. She had been thinking of me and wrote to me before she got my first letter!

There was no other way to communicate except by what we call today "snail mail." Mail to and from *Bangassou* gave a meaning to the phrase that can *not* be fully appreciated by people whose "snail mail" letter arrives at its destination within several days!

I certainly wished for the opportunity to talk to Sallie by phone and hear her voice. In those days there were no phones in that part of Africa – perhaps in the capital city, but not far interior where I was. What about email? This was before the days of email!

So Sallie and I continued to write. Our letters increased in frequency.

My missionary work continued, but I found it more and more difficult to concentrate. Sallie was always on my mind and, increasingly, on my heart.

Over the months, however, I was dismayed to realize that, in spite of the bond we were developing, I was beginning to forget what Sallie looked like. The four days we had overlapped in *Bangui* had been so short that my memory of her appearance was fading.

Writing each other was our only way of communicating

At times, I would stare at the little, wallet-sized, school picture Sallie had sent to me through the mail, trying to recapture the mental image of her that I had retained since the time I kissed her goodbye in the *Bangui* airport. And yet that image eluded me. The school picture taunted me with the face of a stranger, one who bore a fair likeness to the girl I remembered but who failed somehow to recall to my satisfaction the image of the delightful girl I was coming to love.

Long before my short term of fourteen months in CAR came to an end, I came to realize that I was head-over-heels in love with a girl whose face I could hardly remember. I was desperate to see her again.

On Sallie's Side of the Ocean

After my graduation from nursing school I moved to Cedarville, Ohio, where I took selected classes in Bible, missions and Christian education at Cedarville College. I lived off-campus and worked at a hospital in the neighboring town of Xenia. I knew that my interest in

Larry was growing, and I wanted to be prepared if the Lord led me toward a career in missions.

Sallie at graduation from nursing school, 1975

Not the Way People Usually Do It!

As soon as I, Larry, returned to the US after my short term in CAR, I made a mad dash to Cedarville, Ohio – because Sallie was there!

I wanted to see this young lady about whom I had been dreaming for fourteen months! And I had carried home from CAR a few carefully-selected souvenirs that I wanted to give to her.

During the four days Sallie and I had overlapped in CAR fourteen months earlier, there had been no opportunity for a "date." Having just returned to the country, my parents were still searching for the right vehicle to buy. I was a short-termer, on the field for only about a year, so I had no wheels. I didn't know my way around the capital or its environs anyway!

Sallie and I were effectively stranded on the mission station in *Bangui*, unless we accompanied another missionary into town to go shopping with them. Besides, maybe dating at that stage would have been premature, for we were just getting to know each other.

Back in Cedarville now, however, it was time to move the relationship to the next level. So we finally had our first real "date," dinner together at a nice restaurant in a neighboring town.

But this first date didn't happen until *after* I had proposed to Sallie!

Yes, proposed. Along with the other gifts I had bought in Africa for Sallie, I had also purchased a choice diamond that had been mined and cut in CAR.

Sallie Tells the Embarrassing Truth about the Proposal

I remember the evening Larry came to see me in Cedarville. He was staying at the home of a professor, but since I lived in an apartment with two other girls we met at my married sister's apartment.

Larry told me about his time in Africa and presented some gifts he had brought for me. Something else he showed me was a sparkling diamond mounted on a small waxed cardboard. As he showed it to me, he explained that he knew God was calling him back to Africa full-time and he wanted to take a wife with him; he thought he would ask me but he wasn't sure yet. We admired the diamond and then he put it away!

The next day Larry went to several of my classes with me and then we went again to my sister's apartment. I was quite surprised that day when he told me that he was now sure and asked me to marry him!

Larry had not yet met any of my family except my sister in Cedarville, and I had only met his parents for those few days in Africa. We had only corresponded for fourteen months and never dated.

When Larry asked me to marry him, I found myself stammering something about probably saying yes later if I didn't answer now, so ... I guess ... yes.

That was October 31, Halloween.

Larry then asked if we could get married over Thanksgiving. When he makes up his mind he is ready to act. After I said no to Thanksgiving and Christmas break, we agreed to get married March 20, during my spring break from college. We received my parents' consent by phone.

The months before our wedding were quite eventful for both of us. I continued with classes full-time and work part- time. Larry joined part of my family at my grandparents' home for Thanksgiving, but ended up in the hospital that weekend getting his appendix out. We anticipated spending Christmas with my family in New York but God again had other plans. Larry was back in the hospital with peritonitis. When he was finally released he was sent to his sister's in Florida to recuperate and gain back some of the weight he had lost.

Meanwhile, we were still planning a wedding in March. With Larry in Florida, me in Ohio and my parents in New York, we somehow managed a beautiful wedding in Michigan in March. I still don't know how we did it.

11

SHORT-TERM IN AFRICA: 1974 – 1975

Going Back in Time

L arry here. Let's rewind to those agonizing fourteen months of separation from Sallie when I was still single. Between the time that I met her in Africa and the time that I saw her again in America and proposed to her, I had to fulfill the short-term missionary responsibilities in Central African Republic to which I had committed myself.

"Monsieur Larry"

To distinguish me from my father, who was known in CAR as *"Monsieur* Fogle," I became known as *"Monsieur* Larry." We encouraged this. Otherwise, when someone called *"Monsieur* Fogle" Dad and I would never know which of us should answer. Besides I liked the casual sound of it.

Unlike English, most other languages of the world pronounce the letter "a" as *ah*, like in the word "father." This is true for both languages we had to use in CAR – *Sango* (*Sahng-go*), the national trade language, and French, the official language of the country. So my name was pronounced "Monsieur *Lah-rry.*"

The title "Monsieur" would ordinarily be translated "Mister" in English. But I came to realize over time that the title was not commonly applied to men in CAR. Instead, it seemed to be used as a title indicating some respect – something like saying "Sir" in English.

"What Do You Do Out There?"

As I immersed myself in the work for which I had come, I would occasionally get a letter from someone eager to know what kind of work I was actually doing in the heart of Africa. Well, since I already knew the *Sango* language from my childhood, I was able to get involved immediately in the missionary work in two ways: first, teaching in the *Bangassou* Bible School, and second, preaching out among the African churches, often in weekend conferences.

Trying to help the missionaries as much as possible, I taught a full schedule of classes in the four-year Bible school. I got along fine using *Sango* for all my teaching. I relied mostly on sketchy mimeographed notes contributed to the Bible school files by former teachers of the courses I was now teaching, and supplemented those notes as I could along the way.

Every Sunday – and most Wednesdays – I was out somewhere preaching among the African churches, again using the *Sango* language. This was an itinerant ministry: I was scheduled to be at a different place every week. For example, I might speak at a town church in the suburbs of *Bangassou* this Sunday, and at a distant village church next Sunday. The week after that, I might encourage a struggling village *koundou* (small "chapel," not yet organized as a church) out on the main road toward the capital city.

A Bible School Unlike Any in the US

The *Bangassou* Bible School concentrated on producing national pastors and pastors' wives for the African churches. A few would graduate to enter another full-time ministry, such as the work of medical evangelist in our mission hospital or in one of our dispensaries or dental clinics. But most of the men were going to pastor existing churches or plant a new church in some village that needed a gospel witness. Some of these pastors would in time be drawn back to help with teaching and even administration in the Bible schools.

In contrast with Christian colleges in the US, our Bible schools in CAR existed to train pastors and other Christian leaders for full-time

Christian ministry. Because of *extremely* limited personnel, facilities and budget, we could not do everything that larger Christian colleges are able to do in the US. So we took in only those who sensed a real call to full-time Christian ministry.

Men in the Bangassou *Bible School, 1974*
Classroom buildings for men (left) and women in background

Partly because of our limited purpose, our schools were all very small. Year after year, the number of students attending each of our several Bible schools across the country ranged between twenty and forty (ten to twenty couples).

In CAR our accepted practice was to allow only married couples to attend Bible school. There was an assumption that married couples would exhibit more maturity and sense of responsibility than single people, and we wanted only those students who were serious about why they were there and who were by this time fairly stable. In addition, without dormitories and a cafeteria to serve their needs, single students in this culture (especially males) would inevitably begin to rely on help from the married students, adding to *their* burden.

With only married couples attending Bible school, we could be sure that each pastor's wife would have some education so that she would be capable of helping her husband in certain ways in the work of the church. If a young man were to come to school single, it would likely be a sweet but uneducated woman whom he would marry after graduation. Then he would have a ministry partner. But his wife would trail far behind him in her ability to contribute to their ministry together.

Women in CAR typically did not enjoy the same level of education as men. We estimated that men who entered our *Bangassou* school at that time averaged about a sixth grade education, while many of their wives struggled to read and write even the simplest of sentences.

It was impossible to teach the women in the same classes as the men. Either the men would be frustrated because we were going too slowly in class, trying to go at a pace that the women could follow, or the women would be frustrated because we were going too fast, trying to go at a pace which would continue to motivate the men.

So for most of the subjects in our curriculum, we had to teach separate classes for the women. We wished we could have avoided this duplication, but we found it to be absolutely necessary.

It was this kind of Bible school in which I found myself teaching at *Bangassou.*

I started by doing my duty. After all, church leadership training is an important part of the missionary task, and I would do my part. But I discovered that I loved teaching. Now church leadership training became an important part of my own missionary calling.

Churches Unlike Those in the US

Every weekend, and often on Wednesday afternoons, I was out preaching in African churches.

The larger churches, especially those in town, met in permanent buildings of some kind. Over time, they had constructed a simple brick or concrete-block building, with pillars holding up the rafters and aluminum roof. Most buildings had only a half-wall standing between the pillars, which left a huge open "window" to the outside. The ledge of this half-wall provided a great seat for children and teens when the church was packed with an overflow crowd. On such an occasion, even the window seats would be filled!

A larger church in the Bangassou *area,*
crowded for a special occasion

Some of the larger churches had the financial capability to build their walls all the way to the rafters. In an attempt to keep the thieves from stealing their simple wood benches or expensive sound equipment, they installed heavy wooden doors and push-out windows that were secured in the best way they knew how. Best of all, some inserted "windows" in the walls that were nothing but an arrangement of slotted cement blocks. These allowed light to enter, but never thieves!

All of these "windows" provided great access to the wind, dust and blowing rains of rainy season. Of course, they also gave access to outside noises, which were easily heard inside the church: the conversation of people as they passed, the crying of babies, the *tap-tap-tap* of a hammer as someone labored on a nearby house, the sounds of children at play, the honking of cars wending their way through the neighborhood, and noisy goats. *Now don't let yourself be distracted . . . . Keep your mind on the message!*

Few churches could afford to pour a cement floor. We almost always sat in church with a dirt floor under our feet.

Only the town churches had any electricity at all. You knew a church was hooked up to electricity if bare light bulbs were strung strategically around the auditorium. Of course, the presence of the bulbs was no assurance that there was electrical current that day!

In contrast, the smaller village churches often met under temporary grass-roofed shelters. Arriving to preach at such a church, I typically found rough-cut poles sunk in the ground, supporting a roof framework of skinny saplings. A thick covering of dry grass was tied onto this framework with flexible strips of bark to provide the simple building with a grass cap.

The resulting grass roof would surprise you! It protects from the sun and even from the rain. A grass roof keeps a hut relatively cool in the heat of the day. Constructed with good grass, installed properly by an African who knows his business, the roof doesn't leak even in a driving rain! It will, however, deteriorate after several years so will eventually need to be replaced.

Unlike a mud-walled hut, however, the grass-roofed village church is probably not cool. Without any walls at all, the sides of the shelter are wide open to the heat and dust.

A typical, simple church building in the village

A good grass roof keeps the rain from coming through the roof, but it doesn't keep a heavy rain from blowing in from the sides. A gentle rain during a church service is not a problem, but a blowing rain may force the congregation to move from one side of the shelter to the other to avoid getting wet.

The average grass-roofed village church, then, resembles a rustic picnic shelter with a grass roof. Now imagine an uneven dirt floor. Imagine logs laying on the ground in parallel rows for benches. Better than that, how about forked sticks dug into the ground, with reasonably straight wooden poles tied into the forks to serve as benches? Now imagine sitting on those uncomfortable "benches" during worship services, Sunday school classes or Bible studies . . . .

Sometimes in larger town churches, sometimes in small village churches, my itinerant preaching ministry continued. It was fulfilling to know that the Lord Jesus was still building His Church in CAR – and I had a small part in it!

No matter what kind of building they had in which to meet, these dear, unpretentious people came to church. They sang lustily. They prayed emotionally. They listened attentively to my imperfect *Sango* as I preached. And many, even dozens on some occasions, responded sincerely.

"How Long Do You Think It Was?"

Sometime during my short term in CAR, Dad and Mom scheduled a bit of vacation for the three of us. We planned to get away from *Bangassou* and make a brief visit to a number of the BMM mission stations across the country.

In my parents' light-blue Volkswagen Beetle, we followed the dirt roads west through *Kembe* (pronounced *Kem-beh*). At *Bambari* (*Bahm-bah-ree*), we turned north to *Ippy* and on farther to *Bria* (*Bree-uh*).

I remember that road to *Bria*. We were getting farther and farther from civilization. The two-track road stretched on into the distance, across the flat grasslands and rolling hills, through the occasional thickets of stunted trees. The narrow track pointed the way ahead of us to our wilderness destination.

Mom, Larry and Dad before trip to Bria, *early 1975*

Dad had given me the wheel. We didn't dare go too fast. Here and there along the road, patches of sand caused the Volkswagen to fish-tail. But the real danger of this two-track road was in the tall grass growing on the slight ridge down the center of the road. This grass could hide all kinds of objects that could damage the car – a dried anthill, for example, or a solid stick of firewood, or a rock too high for our vehicle to straddle.

We were moving down the road at about thirty miles per hour, I would guess. The road had been surprisingly smooth for the last few miles, and I had yielded to the temptation to pick up a little speed.

Ahead, I focused my attention on a dark line across the road. *What is that?* As the car drew closer, my impression was that it was a small, straight sapling or tree limb five or six inches in diameter. It lay directly across the road, coming out of the grass on the right side of the road and extending at least twelve feet in front of us into the grass on the left.

By now, it seemed too late to stop in time. *No matter – it looks smooth, and small enough that it would not hurt us to run over it.*

Approaching the limb, we were surprised to find it rearing up in front of us! It was a huge snake! It was at least fifteen feet long, for we had not seen either its head or tail as it stretched from the grass on one side of the road into the grass on the other side of the road.

Antagonized by the sound of the approaching engine, the angry python reared up in front of our windshield. With its head at the height of ours, we looked into its eyes for a brief second. And then the snake was slapped down by the steel and glass monster that bore down on it!

I wanted to stop to see if we had killed the snake – and to measure it! – but Dad didn't want to take the time.

After hesitating a moment, I capitulated and pressed on the gas. As we moved on toward *Bria*, however, that python occupied our thoughts. We debated especially one burning question: "How long do you think it was?"

Oh, if only we had stopped . . . .

A Month at **Kaga Bandoro**

In the early months of 1975 I arranged to spend about a month in another part of CAR with my sister and brother-in-law, Maribeth and Don Peterson. They lived at *Kaga Bandoro* (pronounced *Kah-gah Bahn-doh-roh*), the place we had previously known as *Fort Crampel.*

BMM missionaries themselves, Don and Maribeth served our missionary families in CAR by caring for their young children while they were away from home at the MK boarding school. As dorm-parents for a number of youngsters up through eighth grade, Don and Maribeth loved them, nurtured them and in general tried to make their MK experience a positive one – in spite of their separation from their parents.

This dorm was the same one in which I had lived when I was a kid. Now I enjoyed seeing life at the dorm again, but from an adult perspective this time.

It was a lot of fun being with Don and Maribeth – and their "kids" – for that month. But I had two other reasons to be at *Kaga Bandoro* at that time.

Dr. Henry Osborn, my linguistics professor in college, was coming to CAR for a literacy workshop at *Kaga Bandoro*. I had been invited to participate.

Our purpose was to produce a new series of three literacy primers for teaching people how to read. We wanted something more effective than what was currently available in CAR. The primers must be interesting enough to the Africans that they would want to continue to the end of the training. Once they were motivated to learn to read, it would not do for them to stop short of their goal!

I worked with a committee of several missionaries and at least one very capable African man. Dr. Osborn led the committee to develop a cohesive series of true-to-life stories based on the everyday village experiences of three imaginary African characters.

The first and most elementary primer was titled *Bama (Bah-mah)*, as it focused on events in the life of a child by that name. The second primer took its name from its primary character, a woman named *Assita (Ah-see-tah)*. The third presented the adventures of a man called *Kossi (Ko-see)*, so his name became the title of that primer.

Of course, we attempted to develop the reading primers in a progressive way, building one sound upon another, beginning the first primer with short, simple sentences of only two or three words and ending with longer sentences in the third primer.

Literacy Workshop at Kaga Bandoro, *1975*
Left to right: Loie Knight, Larry, Lillian Orton, Joseph Ali, Henry Osborn

Near the end of the workshop, I found another way to help. My motorcycle had accompanied me to *Kaga Bandoro* so that I would be mobile. Using the cycle, I was able to make several day-trips to visit village churches which could not easily be reached by truck. The purpose of these trips was to connect with some of the poor readers in those churches, in order to field-test the new reading lessons that were being developed.

A second reason for my spending some time at *Kaga Bandoro* was to free me from my regular ministry duties at home so that I could complete the doctrinal part of my application for BMM.

At *Bangassou* the responsibilities I had undertaken and the inevitable interruptions I faced where people knew me were beginning to overwhelm me. I was just *not* managing to set aside the concentrated time for doctrinal study that I needed in order to complete my application for BMM. Being away from home allowed me to focus time and energy on that project.

It was satisfying to return to Bangassou at the end of that month away, knowing that I had accomplished what I had intended.

Dad's Guns

Dad had done a lot of hunting during his earlier years in Africa. But now his missionary career was winding down, even as mine was starting. He needed to make some decisions about what to do with the three guns that he owned.

One was an old semi-automatic .22-caliber Winchester that held a clip of seven bullets. This gun was used for small game, including guinea fowl, baboon and small antelope. Dad occasionally shot even larger antelope with this gun, squeezing off two shots. If the first bullet hit its target, the second bullet would follow immediately and finish off the animal.

The second gun was a single-shot .30-30 rifle that was used for bigger game – large antelope, warthog, crocodile, leopard, giraffe and the like.

The third was a powerful .375 rifle, a beautiful gun with gleaming metal and a carved, polished stock. A visiting hunter had left this prize to Dad years before, after Dad had served as his guide for a successful hunt. This gun was reserved for big game, such as elephant, hippo, buffalo and rhino.

Since Dad was planning to make this his last term in Africa, he needed to decide what to do with his guns when he left. He thought he had several options: take the guns back to the US with him, sell them or pass them along to his son. I was all in favor of the third option!

If there was ever a place where a gun would be useful, it was central Africa! I could use the guns to provide some of the meat we ourselves would eat, and by hunting I could also provide some of the meat needed for pastors' conferences, church conferences and youth camps. I wasn't sure I would take the time for big-game hunting, but I *really wanted* Dad's guns – especially his semi-automatic .22!

Before my short term came to an end, Dad began to check on the possibility of passing his guns to me.

At this time, however, illegal hunters were "poaching" the animal population, decimating several animal species. The elephant was one animal that was nearing extinction. Everyday abuse of the hunting laws was epidemic.

Fortunately for the animals but unfortunately for us, the government in CAR was responding to this abuse by tightening the laws. In fact, the officials in *Bangassou* were especially strict in their interpretation of the new laws.

My father asked, "When I leave Africa, can I give my guns to my son and title them in his name?"

"No, new laws do not allow person to give *ngombe* (*ngom-beh*) to another person."

"Can I sell *ngombe* to my son for small price?"

"No, according to law no person is permitted these days to buy or sell *ngombe* in CAR."

"So I cannot *give* my guns to my son, and I cannot *sell* them to him . . . . Can I arrange for my son to get my *ngombe* after I die?"

"Oh, yes, you can do that. But we must hold *ngombe* in storage until your son brings an official certificateof death to prove that you died true!"

What we had discovered was that there was no way I could take possession of Dad's guns except as an inheritance, after Dad's death.

In the meantime, the government administration in *Bangassou* would hold the guns for us. We knew that, until Dad died, it was possible that the guns would be used illegally by corrupt officials. By the time I would take possession of the guns years later, they would probably no longer function!

As it turned out, it would be nineteen years before my father died. If the guns had *not* been used in those intervening years, they would perhaps have been so rusty that they would have never fired again.

Since the new laws also prohibited me from importing a gun from the US, I had to resign myself to the fact that I would never own a gun in CAR. Oh, a pellet gun was permitted, but I would never be able to do any serious hunting.

In the end, Dad made the wise decision to pack up his guns and take them back to the US to sell there. That was the end of the matter. Any hope of getting Dad's guns was gone.

It Wasn't Fair

In fact, the story of Dad's guns does not end here. Several years later, in the middle of our first full term in CAR, I became aware that another missionary MK, now an adult, had managed somehow to gain possession of his father's guns!

Far across the country at *Sibut* (pronounced *Sih-byoot*), Vernon Rosenau and his father approached the local officials seeking to transfer the father's guns to the son. While we had failed to accomplish this at *Bangassou*, the government officials at *Sibut* interpreted the laws differently and allowed the transfer!

So through his years in CAR Vernon used his guns to hunt at will – shooting anything he wanted – while with my pellet gun I could shoot only birds and squirrels. It wasn't fair!

Okay, Larry, get over it. No, it wasn't fair . . . . But don't be bitter about it.

Well, I'm not really bitter, I responded to myself. *More like mildly peeved. All right, seriously peeved!*

Back and forth I went.

10

AN UNUSUAL COURTSHIP

"What Do We Have **Here?"**

My parents and I were picked up at the airport in *Bangui* (pro-nounced *Bahng-ghee*), the capital of the Central African Republic, by one of the local Baptist Mid-Missions missionaries. A couple of young African men sat in the back of his super-cab pickup truck to protect our luggage from potential thieves, while we found seats in the cab.

During the fifteen-minute ride back to the mission property, the missionary commented, "Larry, you might be interested to know that there's a young lady, Sallie Pickard, at the mission right now. Sallie is finishing a six-week missionary apprenticeship with BMM at *Bangassou* (pronounced *Bahng-gah-soo*), the very place where you will be going with your parents. She just arrived this afternoon from *Bangassou*, and will be here for four days until she flies out to return to the US."

Well, so what? I thought. *What kind of girl is willing to come to Africa as a short-term missionary anyway? She won't be the kind of girl who would interest me. Not a chance!*

I had so convinced myself that girls were to be set aside from my thoughts while I was in Africa, I turned my attention to the familiar sights and sounds of Africa and didn't think about this mystery girl again – for a whole twenty minutes.

But it really isn't Vernon's fault that you could only use a pellet gun for those fifteen years in CAR, while he could use his guns for serious hunting.

Of course, I know it wasn't his fault, but . . . he could have hunted less and enjoyed it less, couldn't he? Why did he have to enjoy his hunting so much? It just wasn't fair.

Get over it!

But I wanted a real gun in central Africa. If there was ever a place to hunt, it was in CAR!

Larry, it was not to be.

This inner dialogue has continued off and on for more than thirty years.

And it's still not fair.

In the Village for a Weekend Conference

Often an African pastor scheduled me for a weekend conference, either in the thriving church which he pastored or in a small, struggling *koundou* nearby for which he had taken responsibility. Many of my weekends were therefore spent out in the village.

Two or three Bible school students accompanied me for each of these conferences. I appreciated their companionship, their knowledge of the culture and their advice when dealing with any problems that arose. They smoothed the way before me in so many ways.

In addition, these students provided some help with the teaching and preaching during the conference. Our teaching, for example, would focus on the general subject of "The Local Church" or "The True Follower of Christ." I would outline a series of lessons to be taught during the weekend, and each student would be assigned a couple of sessions. Everyone prepared his assigned lessons in order that our conference would be profitable for the local church.

Our habit was to leave on Friday afternoon after classes were finished for the week. Depending on where this weekend's conference was to be held, we would arrive before the sun went down, or in more distant locations we would pull into the village after dark and unload our things by flashlight.

The conference sessions would begin Saturday morning, with several sessions before lunch and several in the afternoon. Late

133

Saturday afternoon we would join the teen boys of the church in challenging the other teen fellows from the village in a soccer game. We often won that game!

Sunday morning, after the typical African breakfast of tea and bread, we would have a couple more conference sessions on the chosen topic. The first of these sessions would substitute for the Sunday school hour that day, then I would preach the last session during the morning worship service. After an African dinner was served, we would pack up and head home, arriving exhausted but fulfilled.

Now to get ready for our Bible school classes the next morning!

12

FOR THE SAKE OF CHRIST

What Are We Going to Do **Now?**

O ne of my weekend conferences while I was in CAR for my short term was scheduled at the large village of *Ngalakpa* (pronounced *Ngah-lahk-pah*). This village was the site of our most distant church in the area southwest of *Bangassou*. Way out along the river, literally at the end of the road, the drive to this village was difficult at best. And rainy season only made things worse.

Everything was arranged in advance. After Bible school classes ended that Friday, the several selected students joined me in Dad's pickup truck as we began our weekend trip. It took only two hours to travel the forty miles to *Ouango*. From that point on, the dirt road deteriorated badly.

This was the season of the heavy rains. Sometimes we plowed through mud puddles which covered the road to a depth of over a foot. Other times, the grass growing down the center of the two-track road was as tall as the hood of the truck. Where the tall grass at the side of the road was heavy with the water from a recent rain, that grass often leaned over into the road, making it almost impossible to discern the tracks we must follow.

Bridges along a backwoods road like this must be negotiated very carefully. The cement bridges that cross the larger streams are very old, and the dirt approaches are badly eroded – deeply rutted and sometimes quite dangerous.

On the other hand, the bridges crossing the smaller creeks are constructed of rough-hewn timbers laid side by side, lengthwise, across the water. A driver must follow those logs straight across the bridge, making sure his tires don't drop through any gaps between the logs. Of course he assumes that the logs of the bridge haven't been weakened by rot or termites.

Rainy season brings other dangers too. A stream will perhaps be swollen by the rains up to the level of the log bridge. Rushing waters may push one or more of the logs from its position, leaving the bridge impassable by vehicle. Or the water may actually overflow the bridge, making it impossible to see the logs well enough to make a safe passage.

A couple of hours beyond *Ouango* we approached the village of *Yappi* (*Yah-pee*) as the afternoon sun waned. We stopped momentarily to visit the leaders of our BMM church located in this village. But we could not remain long for we still had about thirteen miles to travel, and we really wanted to reach *Ngalakpa* before dark if possible.

Excusing ourselves quickly we moved on through *Yappi* until we confronted the river on the other side of the village. *Oh, no! What are we going to do now?* Some of the large wooden beams crossing this thirty-foot-wide river channel had been dislodged and tossed aside by the swollen waters, and the remaining beams were almost completely submerged!

My Pride Caused Me to React

Pausing to consider our options, we decided we did not dare to attempt to cross with the truck. In frustration we returned through the village to the home of the lead deacon in the *Yappi* church, which had no pastor at the time.

As we debated together what we should do, the several Bible school students expressed their unanimous conclusion. "If not for you, *Monsieur* Larry, *we* would travel on foot to arrive at *Ngalakpa*. People are expecting us there, and we want not to discourage them."

That bothered me a little bit. *As if a white man couldn't walk those thirteen remaining miles with them!*

My pride caused me to react immediately without thinking. "Well, if *you* can travel there on foot, I can travel there on foot same way!" Their looks of skepticism were finally squelched by my insistence that I was in good shape; I could keep up with them.

That decision made, we began to discuss the practical matters related to the long, difficult trek that was ahead of us. The sun was now setting, and it would be foolish to attempt the hike in the darkness of night.

We would have to sleep in *Yappi* overnight. We would leave early in the morning. Others from the church would accompany us to help carry the baggage we needed for the conference. If all went well, perhaps we could arrive in *Ngalakpa* by mid-morning. Even if we started late, we would still be able to hold the conference we had planned.

Unloading the truck for an unexpected overnight in Yappi

The Pile of Stuff was Intimidating

Before dawn people began to gather outside my hut. The baggage had been sorted so that we would have to carry only the bare minimum. Still the pile of stuff was intimidating.

My personal things did not amount to much. I required little more than the Bible school students accompanying me. A change of clothes for the following day. Soap, washcloth and towel. A sheet to throw over me at night.

In addition, all of us had our Bibles, songbooks, and notes for teaching at the conference.

Drinking water was a problem. The missionaries had learned to guard themselves from the parasites that were ever-present in the ground water due to the lack of basic sanitation practices. For my weekend conferences I usually carried a two-gallon thermos and a two-quart thermos of filtered water, plus a quart canteen in the truck available for immediate use.

Although the others in my party were used to drinking the unclean water, I was not willing to risk it. We decided that for our hike I would take only my canteen and the two-quart thermos. Upon our arrival at *Ngalakpa*, I would ask our hosts to boil some river water for me to replenish my supply so I could make it through the weekend.

One more thing: I was committed to carrying Sango Bibles, song-books, Sunday school lesson books and other Christian literature in order to make them available at cost to the folks in the *Ngalakpa* church. The literature which filled a footlocker in the back of the truck was reduced to what could be contained in a smaller box.

Thankfully, our friends were willing to help us carry all this stuff!

I Could Not Do This Any More

By dawn we were on our way. We had grown from a party of four to about fourteen, as men from the *Yappi* church insisted on helping us as porters.

As we started on our way, I noticed that everybody in the group carried something. Anything with a strap hung from the shoulder, while other items were draped over the shoulder to allow the back to bear the weight. Yet other loads were balanced on the head. The weight of the literature box rested on the luggage rack of a bicycle, which would not be ridden but would be pushed all the way because of the hazards of the road.

For my part, my African friends insisted I should carry nothing but my pellet gun. Something about . . . – about my being a respected leader among them.

In their thinking, a leader should not have to bear any burdens. In much of Africa, the traditional pattern of what a leader is and how he acts is the village chief – or even the military dictator who leads their country. His function is not to serve but to be served. Well, that kind of thinking went against the grain for me.

Carefully crossing the remaining beams of the bridge

I started that long hike doing what my companions expected me to do. I was always near the front of the single file, sometimes leading the way. I wore a black cowboy hat to limit my exposure to the sun, and carried my pellet gun on my shoulder.

But I was embarrassed by this colonial display of superiority – you know, the white man leading a long line of burdened black men down the path through one village after another, as if they were his slaves. No . . . , I could not do this any more.

This was an occasion when I could show myself to be a servant. Insisting that I should take my turn carrying something, I traded my gun to a Bible school student. He took my place in front of the line, and I took his load.

A Load on My Head . . . A Smile in My Heart

I had never been able to carry anything on my head like the Africans could. Their hair allowed them to perch a basin of market vegetables or a bundle of firewood on their heads without slipping. The few times I had tried resulted only in disaster – along with hearty laughter from any who had been watching! The long, straight strands of my hair always shifted one way or another, allowing the load to slide off my head. I just couldn't do it.

But now I tried again, expecting that the flat top of my cowboy hat would help me hold my load steady. With the help of my hat, I was delighted to find myself successful! Those in my party could hardly suppress their smiles at first but soon settled into the serious task of putting the miles behind us.

I fell farther back in line as I attempted to keep pace with the others. It did not take long to get the hang of the loose, flowing gait required to keep the load sitting motionless on my head while covering the distance. I felt some pride over my accomplishment. This felt like a small victory.

A couple of miles later we found ourselves emerging from a long stretch of uninhabited wilderness into a small village. Imagine the surprise of the villagers when they saw a line of Africans – *and a white man?* – hiking the road in front of their huts. There was an African in front, carrying a gun, while the white man followed near the end of the line – *balancing a box on his head!*

It seemed that everybody in the village appeared now to view the spectacle. They chattered in their local dialect and pointed at the unbelievable sight.

Some waved. To keep my load from falling I had to keep my head still, so I didn't dare turn my head from side to side to respond. But from the corners of my eyes I saw them waving at me and, without moving my head, I raised my hand in an answering wave and shouted the greeting word in their dialect.

Exiting the village we continued on our way. My companions could not control their mirth. One asked me, "You want to know what people of village said as they chattered among themselves?"

Other friends joined the conversation now, offering their observations all at the same time. "They all said they had seen such a sight never before! They were amazed to see this thing!"

It felt good to join the others in their laughter.

I had managed to carry a load on my head like the Africans – cheating a bit by using my hat, of course! And now I carried a smile in my heart. Yes, this really felt good.

A Blistering Pace

The road we were hiking followed the *Oubangui* (*Oo-bahng-ghee*) River that separated CAR from the country of Zaire. My guess is that we were never more than a half-mile from this major river.

Our first steps that morning had been through water, as we used our feet to feel for the submerged logs of the bridge just outside *Yappi*. But rainy season had swollen not only the smaller streams; the *Oubangui* River had also overflowed its banks, leaving water covering the road wherever the land was low. So the water through which we were forced to wade extended beyond the bridge.

The water on the road was never really deep, never a danger to us. But it seemed to me that the road was under water for at least a quarter of the distance we had to hike. In some places the tall grass on either side of the road appeared instead to mark the boundaries of a small river, a stream that stretched into the distance as far as we could see.

Our trek took us across uninhabited wilderness and through a number of villages. There were lush grasslands dotted with large, mushroom-shaped anthills. There were thick forests. There were rocky hills. But above all there was water, sometimes ankle-deep and sometimes just above our knees.

My fellow-hikers kept up a blistering pace. It took us only about five hours to walk the thirteen miles. This pace was remarkable when you consider the loads we were carrying, the uneven terrain and the water through which we had to wade.

I pushed myself to keep up with the others. And I did. But I will admit that I was really whipped when we arrived at our destination, while my companions hardly appeared to be winded!

"Isn't the River Right There?"

Even though I had forced myself to ration my filtered water, my two-quart thermos was empty by the time we arrived at *Ngalakpa*. I had only my quart canteen to get me through the next hours.

After greeting our hosts, I asked them if they would have someone boil some water for me. I reminded them that to kill the bacteria in the water it is necessary to boil the water for twenty minutes, not just bring it to a boil. After cooling for several hours the water would be sufficiently cool, and I would have all the drinking water I needed to get me back to *Yappi* where I could access the water in the truck.

Since the church folks had been waiting for us we were able to begin our conference almost immediately. Their eagerness to learn was satisfying. Their hospitality was understandably simple but very generous.

One thing did unsettle me a bit that Saturday. I asked to know where their outdoor latrine was.

The African latrine was typically a hole in the ground supported by criss-crossed logs, and surrounded by some kind of small, unroofed enclosure. My hosts looked mystified by the question, then finally responded with a shrug, as if I should have known the obvious answer. "Isn't the river right there?"

As the village stood immediately at the edge of the river, the meaning of their answer was *abundantly* clear.

I asked one of the Bible school students about this later in the day. He clued me in: "They use river water for cooking food, for washing bodies and for washing clothes. They also use river as toilet."

"But what about people of next village down-stream? Don't these practices contaminate river water for *them*?"

"Well, yes. But people of village think about that never."

"And people of next village up-river – do they contaminate river water same way for *this* village?"

"Yes, I'm sure they do."

Ay-ay-ay . . . .

Anyway, we managed to convince our hosts that we would find an appropriate place in the grass away from the river.

Late in the afternoon, I finally received the water they had boiled and cooled for me. My quart canteen had been empty for the last couple of hours, so I guzzled the drinking water until I was finally satisfied.

It wasn't until the next morning that I thought to ask the source of the water they had boiled for me. I should have anticipated the answer that I received: "Isn't the river right there?"

"You Have Strength Much More than Me!"

After one conference session during the Sunday school hour, I preached the morning worship service at the church in *Ngalakpa*. A delicious African dinner followed.

Finally our things were gathered, and we said our goodbyes in preparation for our return trek to *Yappi*.

Ready for the thirteen-mile hike back to Yappi

I confess that I was dreading the hike back. Walking to this river village had been a bit of an adventure. By now, however, the adventure had worn off and the reality of the miles to be covered loomed large in my thinking.

My leg muscles had functioned well enough on the Saturday morning trek, but they stiffened overnight and I woke Sunday morning feeling like I could hardly move. My muscles rebelled at the thought of repeating that Saturday trip only twenty-seven hours later!

Groaning to myself as we took off around 1:00 pm, I tried to hide my discomfort from my hiking companions. Their pace was not much different from that of the day before, and I struggled to keep up. I drifted to the end of the line, and found myself lagging a bit behind the others.

My friends were patient with me and tried to encourage me. But we all knew that even at the same pace as Saturday, dark would be descending on us before we arrived in *Yappi*. None of us wanted to walk this road after dark!

The trek seemed to be interminable! All I could do was force myself to put one foot in front of another and keep going. *Ooooohhh!* How my muscles ached.

Just as night fell like a curtain over the African landscape, we reached the submerged bridge outside the village of *Yappi*. By the dim light of our flashlights, we carefully negotiated those underwater logs and reached the safety of the village. What comfort I took in the kind hospitality offered by the *Yappi* church leaders!

Chatting around the campfire that evening, we re-lived our weekend experience in the hearing of the church folks and other villagers who joined us. We had lots of things to report.

My travel companions wanted especially to relate their observations about *Monsieur* Larry carrying the box on his head through the village and the reaction of the villagers to this amazing sight.

I was very transparent about my inability to keep up with the pace set by my African brothers. "Before this walk, I thought I was strong and could travel on foot same like you. Now I know this is not true! Our going yesterday was difficult not too much, but returning here today was difficult *too much*. These men traveled on foot so fast that I could not keep up with them! I will drive home tomorrow morning, but I will go with new respect for you all in my heart. Yes, I admit it . . . – you have strength much more than me!"

Only If I Had a Vehicle Available to Me

This kind of satisfying ministry was possible, however, only if I had a vehicle available to me that was large enough for transporting the Bible school students and carrying the supplies I needed for a weekend in the village.

Thankfully, my parents had an old gray Chevrolet pickup that I could use when necessary. That truck was the one we had taken on the *Ngalakpa* trip. Dad and Mom did have another vehicle for their own use, a used Volkswagen Beetle that they had bought at the beginning of this term.

I didn't need to use Dad's pickup all the time. After all, I was still single at this time. For my own itinerant preaching schedule, a motorcycle was sufficient to get me around for my meetings among the churches.

13

CROSS-COUNTRY
ON A MOTORCYCLE

"Off-Road" Riding at Its Best

Within the first few weeks of my short term in Central African Republic, it had become obvious to me that a motorcycle would be useful for my itinerant ministry among the churches.

Having just bought a newer Volkswagen Beetle, my parents had planned to let me use the older one they had used their previous term. I could fix it up to use during my short term. But we found that it didn't want to be fixed! In the end we decided it should be sold for what we could get out of it. A motorcycle would meet my needs.

So when my parents made their next trip to the capital for supplies, I hitched a ride with them. In *Bangui* I bought a new Yamaha motorcycle.

The Yamaha I bought was a full-sized "street bike" – really built for city use, not for rough use out on the dirt roads of central Africa. With only a small 50cc engine, the bike was definitely underpowered for the way I was planning to use it but, in fact, it surprised me with how gutsy it was. As a single guy, I knew this motorcycle would do what I needed it to do for the remaining year of my short term.

Hmmm. Now I had a problem. How could I get the Yamaha back to *Bangassou*?

My parents' Volkswagen Beetle could not transport my motorcycle back to *Bangassou*! So I decided it would be an adventure to ride the motorcycle cross-country to get home. Dad and Mom could go on ahead, for they would be able to move along the dirt roads faster than I. My motorcycle was new and reliable. There was no reason for them to wait for me.

The trip cross-country to *Bangassou* was a trip of about 760 kilometers, or just under 500 miles. With four wheels under them, my parents might be able to reach *Bangassou* in two long, hard days of driving. On the other hand, the dirt roads would be a constant challenge to me with only two wheels!

Staying upright on the dirt roads would force me to maintain a slower pace. I would have to remain alert for the occasional ruts that might throw me, or the stretches of "washboard" which could make my teeth rattle and cause me to lose control. Navigating a sandy stretch in the road without falling would test the limits of my strength and skill. Keeping the bike from sliding out from under me when I hit a patch of gravel would require constant vigilance, especially on a curve.

And in each village there would be chickens, goats and dogs to be avoided as they darted into the road in front of me, with no regard for their safety – or mine! If I swerved too suddenly, I could end up on the ground. If I did *not* swerve fast enough, I would injure or kill somebody's animal – and *still* end up on the ground!

This cross-country trip from the capital city to *Bangassou* would prove to take four days by motorcycle. After the first easy day, I would face three days of . . . – well, this is too strong, but "torture" is the word that comes to mind! Three days of tense riding from sunup to after dark. Three days that would test the limits of my endurance.

This was "off-road" riding at its best, although I was never off the road! "Off-road" riding – on the road!

A Remarkable Sense of Adventure

The first day was pretty light. Tying my load of supplies onto the motorcycle's luggage rack, I left Bangui behind and followed the paved road about 125 miles straight north. My goal for that day was the Baptist Mid-Missions station at the town of *Sibut*.

It was a pleasant day and the ride was exhilarating. I felt a remarkable sense of freedom and adventure, being on my own out in the African countryside with the wind blowing on my face. I was in a country I loved, living a life I loved!

This close to the capital city, the higher volume of traffic along the paved road to *Sibut* required me to be especially careful. And I had to be alert for the occasional pothole. Nevertheless, I was able to move along well and I arrived in the outskirts of *Sibut* just before dark. Leaving behind the paved road through town, I took the short-cut, crossed the one-lane bridge and joined the gravel road heading out of town toward *Bangassou*. My goal for the night was just ahead along this road.

In the growing darkness, the lights of the *Sibut* mission could be seen ahead. The mission was situated on top of a rock-and-gravel hill a couple miles outside of town, and its lights served as a beacon to guide me home. Within minutes, I was pointing my headlight up the rough driveway which took me to the missionary homes at the top of that steep hill. As if I were family, the missionaries provided me a welcome meal and a place to sleep for the night.

A Long Day "in the Saddle"

The second day started early, setting the pattern for the next three days. On my way after an early breakfast, I knew I faced a long day "in the saddle."

Leaving Sibut *early on the second day*

Unlike the previous day, I would be all day on dirt and gravel. I had gotten the feel of the motorcycle on the paved road. But it would handle differently on an unpaved road.

The biggest challenge I faced that day was fighting to keep the loaded cycle upright, as the gravel provided a less-than-stable footing for my tires. With loose gravel, any unevenness in the road surface could make the bike slide out from under me. The constant steering adjustments that were required to balance the bike made the ride a tense one.

Choosing where to place my tires on the road was not a simple matter. On a one-lane dirt road, the occasional traffic wore two tire tracks in the surface, which eventually became two slight troughs in the dirt. Some of the gravel displaced by the tires was spit toward the outside edges of the road, while an equal amount of gravel was thrown toward the center, eventually growing into a hump in the middle of the road. In the resulting "two-track" road, the center hump was sometimes covered with a growth of grass.

It was slow going. At times, I would guide my cycle down the left track of the road – until a rut or a patch of sand or a stretch of "washboard" would force me over to the track on the right. However, navigating that center hump of gravel on the road had to be done with great care! It could only be done safely by slowing down and exercising great caution. Otherwise, I would end up on the ground.

My goal that second day was roughly 125 miles from *Sibut* – the BMM station at *Bambari*, the second largest city in the CAR.

I don't mind admitting I was tired by the time I pulled into the mission driveway after dark. In addition, I was gaining a new respect for anybody who could sit for hours at a time on a motorcycle – at least on this kind of road. There's no polite way to say this . . . . My bottom was getting sore!

How Could I Be So **Stupid?**

My third day on the road would take me another 125 miles along the road to our next mission station outside the town of *Kembe*. I knew this day would be a real challenge, for the roads became progressively worse the farther one traveled from the capital.

I started the day at sunup, already tired and sore. About half-way to *Kembe*, the road passed through *Alindao* (*Ah-lin-dah-o*), a fairly large town in the grasslands. *So far, so good*, I thought to myself. I was relieved to have made it this far without problems.

I allowed myself to pause at the open market, to get off the motorcycle and stretch. Buying some fresh fruit, I devoured it on the spot.

About ten miles past *Alindao*, approaching a flat, grassy plain, the back of my bike began to weave back and forth. Realizing that I had a puncture, I slowed to a stop. Repairing a flat on a motorcycle is not as easy as it is on a bicycle, but with the help of the tire patch kit that came with the cycle, I managed to repair the puncture and pump up the tire. *On my way again!*

But I did not get far. Within five minutes the cycle was weaving again. By the time I stopped this time, the rear tire was entirely flat. Pulling the inner tube out of the tire, I found . . . *Oh, no! Stupid me! I had forgotten to remove the nail that had caused the* first *puncture, and by now that nail had made ten fresh holes in the inner tube!*

Needless to say, I had a problem on my hands. My one remaining patch and glue took care of only one of the ten punctures. *Now what was I going to do? How could I be so* stupid?

The sun blazed hot, high in a cloudless sky. As I considered my predicament, discouragement set in.

Before long, an African man came along on his bicycle. We greeted each other and he stopped to ask about my problem. Explaining that I had already used all my patches and all my glue, I asked what the Africans did to repair *their* tires – for I knew they didn't always rely on the expensive tire repair kits of the *moundjou* (*moon-joo*, meaning "white man").

"Oh, for a patch we just use a piece of rubber from the inner tube of a bicycle . . . . Here, take this extra strip of inner tube rubber and cut it into small pieces for patches."

"Thank you very much! And . . . for glue, what do you use?"

"For glue we just use the sap of a tree. Oh, not just the sap of any tree. There are just certain trees whose sap is very, very sticky and will dry like glue." Looking around, he finally pointed to a small thorny tree out in the grass, about fifty yards from the side of the road. "There," he pointed. "That tree there . . . If you will use your knife and cut into its bark, you will make the sap come out. That is what you can use for glue."

As my new friend continued on his way, I did as I had been told. The inner tube rubber was cut into a number of small patches. Then I made my way through the tall grass to the thorn tree that had been pointed out to me, and with my pocketknife dug into its bark to release its sap. Cradling the sap carefully on a leaf, I brought it back to the motorcycle and began the tedious job of fixing the tire I had ruined.

Finally, with a sigh of relief, I was back on the road again.

But . . . *Wait! Don't be too quick to think your problems are all behind you!*

Unfortunately, within ten miles my tire again went flat. One of my new patches had come off. I had to find some more sap and replace the patch.

I traveled another five miles before another patch failed.

For the rest of the trip, every five or ten miles, over and over and over again, I had to stop to repair a flat tire. I could go only so far before one of my patches let go. I respected the Africans for using what local means they could to repair their bicycle tires. But I now understood that a simple, "home-remedy" repair that would support the weight of a bicycle would *not* adequately support the weight of a motorcycle!

The remainder of my trip stretched out long in front of me. I knew that I was not likely to find any other "professional" patches and glue before I reached *Bangassou*.

My progress was excruciatingly slow. Long after dark, I limped into our mission at *Kembe*. I was exhausted and discouraged, but at the same time satisfied to have arrived this far on my way home!

"Do You Love Jesus?"

One more day to go! Only about 110 miles left to *Bangassou*.

By the end of that fourth day I should be home. But getting back on the Yamaha early that morning . . . It was almost more than I could force myself to do.

Working on the troublesome tire – still no proper patches!

The repeated flats and repairs continued to slow my pace. There was still no way to do a proper repair of my rear tire.

Each small town through which I passed gave me some hope that I might find some real patches and glue. But with no auto parts stores or repair garages around, I could only hope that one of the "shade-tree mechanics" might have what I needed. But over and over again I was disappointed. "Sorry, I used my last patches and glue earlier this week. Maybe you will find some in the next town along the road."

The torturous trip continued through the long, hot day. I still had about 45 miles to go when, just as the darkness of night was settling around me, I entered the outskirts of the large village of *Gambo* (pronounced *Gahm-bo*). Here, once again, my rear tire began to weave under me. *Oh, no! Here we go again . . . .*

As I squatted by my back tire to pull out the inner tube and identify the current leak, an African man approached, going in the same direction as I was. His old bicycle staggered under the enormous load tied onto its luggage rack. Seeing I was having a problem, the man carefully leaned his bicycle over into the grass at the side of the road. Coming near, he squatted beside me. We chatted as I continued to work on my tire repair.

It did not take long to recognize that this guy was drunk as a skunk. He slurred his words and, in addition, his breath smelled heavily of whiskey.

I had never drunk alcohol of any kind – it did not attract me and I was aware of its dangers. But I knew what homemade, African palm liquor smelled like. And this guy had drunk more than his fair share!

You see, squatting together in the dirt of the road, our faces were at times only twelve inches apart. It was clear to me that this man had been drinking. Every time he opened his mouth, I was repelled by the disgusting odor of the palm liquor. My natural inclination was to turn away from him, to reject any further association with him.

Instead, I turned the conversation to spiritual things. "*Monsieur*, I want to talk with you about very important person. His name is Jesus. He is very important because He is Son of God and Savior of the world. Do you know this Jesus?"

"Oh, yes! I have taken baptism!"

"Sir, I didn't ask you if you have taken baptism. I asked you if you know Jesus. Tell me how you know Jesus."

"Well, this large village of *Gambo* we are entering . . . There is church in this village, *Gambo* Baptist Church. I took baptism in that church and I am member of church!" His words were slurred.

"You are member of that church? True words?"

The drunk replied, "Oh, yes. That is my church!"

"And do you attend church there regularly?" I pushed him further.

"Well, no, I go there not every Sunday," he admitted. "But it is my church!"

I was familiar with *Gambo* Baptist church, for it was one of the area churches that was loosely affiliated with Baptist Mid-Missions and I had preached there.

My mind was processing the drunk's claims about his relationship with the church. *This man may have been baptized in that church some time in the past, but he has not been a real part of the church for a long time.* It was time to challenge him.

"I have heard that this church recently called new pastor to lead them. What is name of your new pastor?"

"Oh, yes, I know new pastor. He is good friend of mine!" He raised his hand in emphasis, but then let it drop slowly as he struggled to come up with the pastor's name. "Wait . . . . I know him well . . . . He is good friend . . . . But I can remember his name not right now!"

"Is his name not Pastor *Yango* (pronounced *Yahng-go*) George?"

"Oh, yes, that is his name," he confirmed loudly, nodding his head with erratic movements.

"Sir," I continued, "I am familiar with *Gambo* Baptist Church. Before they allow someone to be baptized and join church as member, I know that they require people to come to Jesus Christ in faith and repentance. You see, they must first believe in Jesus as their Savior and commit themselves to Him as their Lord. Have you believed in Jesus like that?"

"Oh, yes . . . . I have believed in Jesus." His mind was not clear. Again he returned to his original declaration, "I tell you I have taken baptism! I am member of church!"

How am I going to get through to him? I guess I need to be more direct. "You say that you have believed in Jesus. You say you have taken baptism. You say you are member of church. But now tell me: Do you drink palm liquor?"

My new friend was now embarrassed. Looking down at the ground, he finally acknowledged the truth. "Yes, I do drink."

"It is obvious, my friend. Smell of liquor is very strong on your breath. I am puzzled by this. You claim to be believer of Jesus, but you drink liquor. This is not way of true believer."

God brought a verse to my mind. I quoted Jesus' words from John 14:15, "If you love me, keep my commandments."

Looking directly into the eyes of the drunk man, I spoke gently, "*Monsieur*, Jesus loves you. That is why He came from heaven to this earth and died on cruel cross. He loves you so much that He took punishment for your sin. He did this so you can receive God's forgiveness and experience His peace. In response to His love, true believer will also love *Him* and want to live for Him."

We were still squatting in the dirt of the road. Nobody else passed to distract us. The repair of my flat tire was all but forgotten. The darkness had settled around us in earnest. Even from twelve inches away, I could now hardly see the drunk's face.

Now, with a serious question, I zeroed in on this unlovable man whom God loved. "My friend, do you love Jesus?"

Again, the drunk looked down at the ground. The silence stretched on, as he found himself unable to answer.

"Thank you for not lying to me. If you had answered me by saying, 'Oh, yes, I love Jesus,' I would have told you that you were liar. You see, in John 14:15 Jesus said, 'If you love me, keep my commandments.' Obedience is what Jesus expects of everybody who truly loves Him. If we do not keep his commandments, we demonstrate that we love Him not truly. My friend, if Jesus is truly your Savior, you must also recognize Him as your Lord, give Him your life and seek to obey Him in all that you do."

We both needed to get home. The African agreed to let me pray for him before we separated. After I prayed for him, I counseled him to meet with Pastor *Yango* very soon. Then I helped him stand his loaded bicycle upright so that he could mount. He was still drunk but hopefully somewhat sobered as he continued on his way.

I turned my attention back to my situation. In the darkness I fished around for my flashlight and debated what to do. Tired and sore, I decided the best thing to do would be to put the inner tube back into the tire, then push the motorcycle through *Gambo* to the church. There I could ask for help from Pastor *Yango*.

About 7 pm, I wrestled the heavy bike up the last hill to the pastor's house. I was so relieved to find him at home!

"It's Just Me – Larry!"

To be sure, I was thankful to be as far as *Gambo*. But I still didn't know how I would arrive home that night. I was to teach in the *Bangassou* Bible School the next morning, but I didn't know how I could go on. I really felt like I was at the end of my strength.

Pastor *Yango* suggested, "Maybe you don't have to continue by motorcycle. Maybe you could get a ride to Bangassou in a truck. If a truck comes by, maybe they would let you *and* your motorcycle ride in the truck."

That sounded like a good suggestion to me. I could not bring myself to get back on that motorcycle that night!

Pastor *Yango* sat with me in the darkness out by the road – waiting, hoping that a truck would come along to help me on my way. All was quiet. No vehicles passed from *either* direction. *God, please send us a vehicle to help.*

Just before 8 pm we heard the distant whine of an engine. Soon we saw a bobbing swath of light moving in our direction, as a truck's headlights pierced the night. Pastor *Yango* waved the loaded seven-ton Mercedes-Benz to a stop and, over the sound of the rough idle of the engine, explained our situation. Before long, the motorcycle was strapped tightly to the top of the truck's huge load, which was heaped several feet above the stake-body frame of the truck.

Clambering atop the truck's load, I found a place to sit where I thought I would be somewhat comfortable. Not wanting to be thrown off the truck, I firmly gripped one of the truck's tie-down ropes with each hand. And off we went.

The heavily-laden truck waddled down the road, with the beams of its headlights pointing the way. The other passengers, seated toward the front of the bulging load, had often ridden in such a way. They seemed to have no problem balancing on top of the load. Farther back on the truck, I hung on for dear life!

Low on the horizon ahead of us, the moon shone bright. The other passengers ahead of me were clearly silhouetted against the light of the moon. Swaying back and forth with the lurching of the truck over the rough dirt road, the erratic movements of the passengers seemed to take the form of a wild dance.

A gourd full of African palm liquor was passed around and lifted to their lips. A second round of drinks . . . and a third. Inevitably, due to the jerky motion of the truck, not all of the liquor made it into their mouths. The rush of wind occasionally blew a spray of the liquid backward at me, and soon my face and clothing stank of the disgusting stuff!

Some of the passengers became quite drunk. I think that's when the singing started – the typical off-key and boisterous singing of a bunch of drunks.

Those several hours on the back of that truck were about as miserable as my last two days on the motorcycle had been. But at least we were moving!

About 11 pm, the truck turned off the main road just outside *Bangassou* to labor up the long mission driveway. Up through the Bible school student village and further up the hill toward the missionary homes.

Everybody was long since in bed, but nobody could stay asleep through the noise we made! *Whose big truck was this that growled and ground its way tediously up the long incline? Who were these people who insisted on waking everybody up by calling to each other and singing at the top of their lungs?*

At the top of the hill, the offending truck staggered to a stop in front of the house I indicated. The several night guards gathered near as Dad stepped outside the door of our house. He had obviously pulled on his housecoat in a hurry. Dad quickly took charge. "Who is it?" he called out in *Sango*.

As I started to untie the ropes holding my motorcycle in place, I answered loudly over my shoulder, "It's just me – Larry!"

Well, my parents had been expecting that I might arrive sometime that day. But they hadn't expected me to arrive so late at night, in the company of such a rowdy bunch – and smelling like a drunk too!

My mind was fuzzy with exhaustion. *It's so hard to think . . . . I made it home . . . . I can finally relax . . . . Too tired to shower tonight . . . .* I cleaned up the best I could with a washcloth and – *finally* – collapsed into bed.

Oh, Yes, Loads *of Fun*

It seems that every time I tell this story, someone wants to tell me, "Oh, I would love to ride a motorcycle on a road like that! That would be so much fun!"

Oh, yes, *loads* of fun.

The trip *did* start as an adventure. It was fun for the first day! And for part of the second also. Then the travel lost its excitement and became a chore. Now the motorcycle was just a way to get to my destination. I just wanted to get there! The third and fourth days were a difficulty to be conquered, a test to be endured.

14

FINALLY A REAL MISSIONARY!

There is No Shortcut

My fourteen-month short term had been completed and, back in the US now, Sallie had agreed to marry me. As much as we were looking forward to our future wedding, however, we needed to concentrate on our responsibilities in the present.

Sallie was fully occupied with her studies at Cedarville College and her part-time nursing jobs. As for me, by this time I had completed all the required papers and was ready to move forward with my application to Baptist Mid-Missions for appointment as a full-time missionary.

Of course, with our wedding planned for March of the next year, we discussed the possibility of my waiting until Sallie and I could join BMM together. In the end, the Mission encouraged me to proceed with my doctrinal examination in November 1975 as scheduled. Then Sallie would take the required steps to join the Mission after we were married.

Completion of a thorough doctrinal questionnaire is one of the requirements for application to BMM. If everything looks fine, an oral doctrinal examination is scheduled. Meeting with the General Council of BMM for this examination is an intimidating prospect. It is much like an ordination council!

How does a missionary candidate prepare to respond to the questions that will be posed by the General Council? There is no shortcut.

Adequate preparation demands concentrated study of his carefully-worded doctrinal statement, so he will be prepared to defend it. He must also memorize numerous Scripture references, which he will need to use in order to support his doctrinal convictions.

As Comfortable as Possible Under the Circumstances

The tension encountered by the missionary candidate is palpable as he or she steps into a room full of pastors, missionaries and other godly people and seeks to respond to their doctrinal questions. As members of the governing council of the Mission, these people hold the power to approve the candidate for missionary ministry or to deny him that privilege!

I found, however, as every missionary candidate does in his turn, that these wise council members are kind and gracious. Yes, they have a responsibility to perform. They must verify that the candidate knows the Scriptures, that he can verbalize what he believes. But they understand that the candidate is nervous, and they go out of their way to make him as comfortable as possible under the circumstances.

This doctrinal examination lasts one or two hours – depending on how many missionary candidates there are to examine, which members of the General Council are assigned to this particular examination and any weaknesses that are discovered in the course of the examination.

What relief it is to the candidate when, finally, someone on the examination council speaks up to say, "Mr. Chairman, I move that the questions cease," and all in favor register their vote by saying, "Aye." The candidate is now dismissed to allow the council members to deliberate. They record their findings and their conclusion about the candidate whom they have examined. Then meeting together with the full General Council, they make their official recommendation about accepting the candidate. The General Council vote is usually taken with great enthusiasm and praise to the Lord!

Occasionally a candidate is deferred until a later time, with some conditions to be fulfilled – often including re-examination at a later meeting of the Council. This is always a possibility, but is in fact quite rare. You see, the BMM administration will ordinarily not bring the candidate before the Council until they are quite satisfied that the candidate is well prepared.

It is even more rare that a candidate is definitely rejected – this would probably indicate that some new information has surfaced that disqualifies the candidate.

Meanwhile, while the General Council discusses their findings, the ordeal is almost over for the prospective missionary. He breathes easier now, but he cannot relax completely until the chairman of his examining council finds him and communicates the decision of the General Council.

"I have the happy privilege of telling you," the candidate is told, "that the General Council has officially voted for your acceptance as a BMM missionary – pending, of course, the usual steps that you will have to take toward appointment!"

The Council spokesman often finds something to compliment about the candidate's performance: "We are especially pleased with your knowledge of the Scriptures, as demonstrated by the verses you offered in support of your doctrinal convictions." Or, "We know you were really feeling stressed. But we were impressed with your composure as you responded to our questions." Or, to a couple, "We were delighted to see how you interacted together as husband and wife when you were in that difficult situation. Your love and patience for each other were plain to see, as you encouraged and supported and helped each other."

Finally, the pressure is off. If there are any more tears, they are tears of joy and emotional release. Now the candidate can relax and just enjoy the rest of the BMM conference. He can sleep that night!

My Weakness Was My Excellent Preparation

My intention was to be as well prepared for my meeting with the General Council as possible. My doctrinal statement had been carefully written. It included plenty of Scripture references to support each point.

Now, as the date for my examination approached, I gave myself seriously to study. As I studied I came to realize, *I really agree with what I have written . . . . Hmm, I guess it's a good thing I do, since I have to defend what I believe!*

I studied so much that I nearly memorized the pages of that doctrinal statement, with every point and every Scripture reference. In fact, that was what concerned my examination council about me: "It seems that he can produce from memory everything on his doctrinal statement. But can he respond to questions and talk about what he believes *aside from* those memorized statements?"

Because of this concern, the chairman of my examination council tried every way he could to ask his questions in a way that would make me divert from my precise, memorized statements.

Ironically, my weakness was my excellent preparation. I was cautioned that temporary memorization of the facts cannot substitute for a long-term comfortable familiarity with the truths of the Word of God.

No Longer a Short-Termer

For every prospective missionary, passing the General Council examination is another step in the application process toward being a full-fledged missionary. Candidates then have to attend Candidate Seminar the following summer before they can officially call themselves missionary "appointees."

In my case, however, the Mission had suggested that I attend Candidate Seminar the summer before I went to the Central African Republic for my short term in 1974-1975. You see, I was planning to join the Mission full-time anyway after that short term, and Candidate Seminar would help prepare me for a fuller, more satisfying involvement with the missionaries, the nationals and my short-term ministries while in CAR.

Having already fulfilled the requirement of Candidate Seminar, I was therefore immediately appointed as a full-fledged missionary appointee.

For me, this was the fulfillment of a life-long dream! I was no longer just an MK. No longer just a short-termer. Now I was a *real* missionary! This marked a new phase in my life.

15

A TERRIBLE FIRST IMPRESSION

My New Family

Now it was time to meet Sallie's relatives – those who would become my new family. Accompanying Sallie to her grandparents' home in Wixom, Michigan, for Thanksgiving would give me the opportunity to meet most of her immediate relatives.

Sallie had just a few days of vacation from school and work. We drove together in my car to join the rest of her family at the home of her grandma and grandpa. Their house, though old and tiny, had a warm, comfortable feel to it and served as a magnet for the family, who knew they were welcome there and flooded in from every direction.

At this point, I had not even met Sallie's parents! Fortunately, they were able to make the trip from New York to be with the family for Thanksgiving. Otherwise I might not have met them until just before our wedding the following March.

One of Sallie's three sisters was there for this occasion, along with many of her uncles, aunts and cousins. For me it was a confusion of people to whom I was introduced for the first time.

Nobody in Sallie's family really knew what to expect of me. To most of them, an MK was a bit of an unknown. Overall, I don't think they were too pleased about this strange young man who planned to marry Sallie and take her off to live in the middle of Africa! Yet they were all kind enough to accept me and our engagement. In response to their acceptance, I have come to love them more and more through the years.

The Pickard family at our wedding the following year, March 1976
Left to right: Front row – Mom, Bonnie Ephraim, Sallie, Larry, Dottie Sergeant;
Back row – Dad, Bill Ephraim, Kim, Wayne Sergeant

When the news had spread through the family the previous year that Sallie was corresponding with a young man she met in Africa, it had been Grandpa who insisted on asking the hardest questions about this young man. Now, meeting Grandpa for the first time, I was a bit intimidated by his bluntness. But as I got to know him better I found out that he had an extremely kind and generous heart.

Until Grandma and Grandpa Wagnitz, I didn't know anything of a child's close attachment to his loving grand-parents. I had never experienced that kind of relationship with anyone, since I never knew my own grandparents.

Grandma and Grandpa Wagnitz took me in as a young adult and became the only grandparents I had ever really known. Sallie's grandparents became mine in a way more meaningful than they could ever have known. I wish now that I had made a point of expressing to them my deep appreciation for that before they passed away.

Grandpa and Grandma Wagnitz, about 1975

The Only Thanksgiving Dinner I Ever Refused

Thanksgiving Day, Grandma and the other ladies in the house did some serious cooking. But during the night, I had become increasingly nauseated and by morning I was pretty miserable. By noon the nausea was overwhelming, accompanied now by an agonizing stomachache. The delicious smells coming from Grandma's kitchen did not interest me in the least. When Sallie bent over me to tell me that dinner was on the table, I told her not to let them wait for me – I didn't want to eat anything.

Anyone who knows me well would know that if I said that, I was really sick! That was the only Thanksgiving dinner I ever refused!

I was no better by the next day, so Sallie's family decided to call the doctor. They were advised to take me to the hospital emergency room right away. There the diagnosis was appendicitis, and I was rushed into surgery where my appendix was removed.

The hospital was still my home when Sallie's weekend break for the Thanksgiving holiday ran out. One of her cousins gave her a ride back to college, even as the rest of her family returned to their homes.

Poor Grandma and Grandpa were left responsible for their new "grandson" who remained in the hospital. They visited me until I was released, then took me home with them to recuperate. To this day I don't know what they did about my hospital and surgery bills. All I know is that I never saw a bill and never had to pay a penny.

16

OUR AMAZING GOD

God's Timing Was Perfect

Eight days after my appendectomy, I left the home of Sallie's grandparents in eastern Michigan to drive about five hours to Mishawaka, Indiana. I had to get there because the next day, Saturday, my home church was convening an ordination council to consider my qualifications for the ministry. If approved by the ordination council, I was to be ordained by my church on Sunday evening, December 7.

These plans had been made months before, in order to take advantage of my preparation for my doctrinal examination by BMM. Why not coordinate that event with my ordination council, so that my preparation for the one event could also help me be prepared for the other?

First Baptist Church of Mishawaka and my pastor at that time, Pastor Glenn Crabb, were satisfied to proceed toward my ordination because I had already been active in full-time ministry for some time and they knew my testimony.

So it was that a group of pastors and church leaders, called by my home church, met with me on Saturday at the designated time.

Knowing that I was still weak from my surgery, the gentlemen allowed me to sit to respond to their questions, instead of standing as was the custom at that time. As I recall, the questioning continued for two and a half hours, before we stopped for a late lunch together.

It was a tiring day, but by the grace of God I managed to do what I had to do: I stated my doctrinal convictions before the council and fielded their questions.

I guess the council members were satisfied because they officially recommended me to the church for ordination. So the following day, in a sobering Sunday evening service, I was ordained.

Larry's ordination at First Baptist Church, Mishawaka IN, 1975
Larry (middle) with participants in ordination service –
Pastor Glenn Crabb at left, former pastor Roy Hamman just behind Larry

To be honest about it, I don't remember much about the ordination service that Sunday evening. However, I certainly do remember what happened later that night . . . .

My parents were still in Africa at the time. In my home town for my ordination, I was staying at the house of Aunt Helen Scanlon on Jefferson Street. Aunt Helen was my father's sister, a godly woman, a genuine prayer warrior! She had prayed for my parents throughout their years in central Africa, and now she had taken on the commitment of praying for her nephew Larry in the same way.

I drove home to Aunt Helen's house, got ready for bed and let myself collapse. It had been an exciting day at church.

Resting in bed, I suddenly experienced an unbearable pain in my abdomen, the kind of pain that makes your body go rigid and makes you grit your teeth and pant for breath. It seemed to me this is what it would feel like if someone were stabbing me with a knife!

The pain did not subside, so I cried out for Aunt Helen. She called 911 and a few minutes later, ten days after my appendectomy, I was hustled off in an ambulance for what would prove to be a month-long stay in the hospital.

God's timing was so perfect! God allowed me to drive to Indiana on Friday, complete my examination by the ordination council on Saturday, interact with my home church all day Sunday and enjoy my ordination service on Sunday evening – all according to His plan – before He would permit a growing infection in my body to come to the point of crisis!

I Flapped My Sheets Like a Crazy Man

From the emergency room, I was immediately admitted to St. Joseph Hospital. The diagnosis this time was "peritonitis." Evidently, there had been some leakage from my infected appendix before it was removed in Michigan. The doctors discovered that in the ten days since my appendectomy this infection had spread, to the point that my abdomen was now one big abscess of infection.

There should have been symptoms of this growing infection before now, such as pain or fever. That such a mass of infection did not bother me at all until that night amazed the doctors! The only possible reason, of course, was God.

For sixteen days, I was not allowed to eat or drink anything. Nutrition was provided for me intravenously. Sucking on ice chips offered some relief when my mouth was dry.

From the beginning of my hospital stay, the medical staff pumped antibiotics into me, in an effort to conquer the infection in my body. From day to day, they evaluated whether or not they should do surgery to clean out the infection. Their concern was that I was still too weak from my previous surgery to undergo another one.

During my first two weeks in the hospital, I slept most of the time – thanks to the pain medication they gave me. When I was awake, I visited briefly with family members and visitors who came to see me. But soon the pain overwhelmed me again and I called the nurse to give me my next dose. Within minutes I sank into a deep sleep again, oblivious once more to the pain – and to my visitors.

Family members later told me that I was sometimes barely coherent during the moments I was awake. I raved about this subject or that and flapped my sheets like a crazy man.

Dr. Raymond Buck, at that time the President of our Mission, stopped one day to visit me in the hospital when traveling through the area. According to the report of one who was present, I talked to my special visitor for only a moment before the required pain medication took me away to a land where he could not go. Dr. Buck understood the circumstances and left quietly. As for me, I did not even remember his visit.

I could have died anytime during those days. I could have drifted away into eternity without any awareness that my life on earth was ending. I understand that my relatives saw my struggle for life and questioned the treatment I was receiving. *Why didn't the doctors just do surgery and get rid of the infection once and for all?* Some in my family even considered contacting my parents in Africa to suggest that they come home to see me before I slipped away.

Slowly, slowly, the antibiotics gained ground and the infection faded. Slowly, slowly, my strength began to return.

After sixteen days of intravenous feeding I was put on a liquid diet, then later on a bland diet. Of course, my stomach had shrunk, so I had very little appetite at the beginning. Two or three bites at a time were all I could manage.

"You Don't Suppose He's Stealing *the Money, Do You?"*

As I regained strength, the hospital staff began to prepare me for my departure.

A lady from their business office visited me to find out how I was going to pay the bill for their services. "Including costs for x-rays and lab work, medications and payment for your room and meals, your total bill is going to amount to over $6,000. We need to know how you are going to pay this bill."

I was staggered to hear the total bill! *How would I ever pay a bill like that?* (Of course, today the cost for a stay of thirty-one days in the hospital would be many times this amount, but this was a huge amount in those days.)

"Well, honestly, I don't *know* how I will pay such a bill."

"Do you have any insurance?"

"No, I don't. Our Mission has a group medical insurance policy, but I have not chosen to enroll in the plan yet. I was going to do that when I get married next spring, so my wife and I both could have that insurance."

"That's unfortunate . . . . Do you have a job?"

"No, I'm a missionary just recently returned from Africa, and preparing to go back overseas again as soon as possible. As a missionary I am trusting God to provide for my needs through the financial support churches will give me. They send money to my Mission for me, and I can use what comes into my account."

"Do you have enough money in that account now to pay your bill?"

I explained my situation as a beginning missionary, with committed support at this time of only $300 per month. "Of course, that money is quickly used each month."

The lady from the business office was persistent. "So how do you plan to pay your bill?"

"I really don't know. God will provide. I'll bring in the money a little bit at a time until I have paid it all."

Anybody could have seen that the lady was quite skeptical as she returned to the business office with my answer.

Upon my release, I wrote a letter to my family, friends and supporters to explain the situation and to ask them to pray. Money – even some from individuals unknown to me – began to come into my BMM account.

Before a week was over, I stepped into the business office at the hospital to present them with the first $600 to apply to my bill. I made another payment before I left town.

Again and again over the following weeks, I sent them more money in varying amounts – $300, $1,100, $800, etc. Within two months, the total bill of over $6,000 was erased!

I'm sure that this was a real testimony to the staff at St Joseph Hospital. Those folks were sure skeptical about my ability to pay the bill by trusting God. Of course, their skepticism may have been more a lack of faith in me and my commitment to pay the bill, than a lack of faith in God's ability to provide!

In any case, the hospital staff were sure surprised to see how quickly this poor Baptist missionary came up with the money to cover his bill! I've always wondered what they said among themselves in that business office after I sent in another payment, and especially after I paid off the entire bill. I can only imagine the conversation that took place.

"Where do you suppose he's getting all that money? He said he doesn't have a regular job."

"I sure don't know where he's getting it! He only has an income of about . . . $300 per month, didn't he say? You don't suppose he's *stealing* the money, do you?"

Through this story of God's amazing provision, Sallie and I were reminded of God's promise to provide for His servants and His work. What wonderful reassurance this was to us, as we considered the financial support we would need to go to Africa! The same amazing God who provided for my hospital bill would continue to provide for our needs.

An Emaciated, Stooped Old Man

Upon my release from the hospital, I stayed in northern Indiana for only a short time. As soon as I was able, I flew to Florida to recuperate.

I had lost about 40 pounds in the hospital. My weight was down to 120 pounds. My appearance was that of an emaciated, stooped old man. My doctor suggested that I go stay with someone in Florida, where I could be outside a little bit each day throughout the winter. The fresh air and the sun would do me good. I would recuperate faster.

Further, the doctor told me to eat in order to gain some weight. "Eat anything you want, as much as you want!" he prescribed. Now that was an order that I was willing to obey!

My sister Lois and her family kindly took me into their Florida home for about two months and fed me well. I gained some weight as my appetite returned. My family noticed that, at meals, I now asked for a second or third helping. "The way you're eating, it doesn't look like you're sick any more," someone said.

In response I could always say, "But the doctor said . . . You know I have to follow the doctor's orders!" It was a convenient excuse for continuing to eat everything I wanted.

Another warned me: "You shouldn't keep eating so much. If you keep eating like this, you will gain back *too* much weight. This way you're going to get *fat!*"

17

CHALLENGES AND BLESSINGS: 1976 – 1977

A Four-Month Honeymoon

As I slowly recovered my health, weight and energy in Florida, I was in regular contact by phone with Sallie who was still in college in Ohio. This long-distance planning for our wedding in Michigan was not the easiest way to arrange the details for a wedding. But Sallie organized everything well and all the details fell into place.

I left my idyllic retreat in Florida early in March, just two weeks before our wedding. Plans were finalized and last-minute details were cared for.

It was only then that I could order my tux, because until then I could not have known what size to order. I had regained about twenty pounds of the forty that I had lost. However, I was still about twenty pounds shy of my normal weight. That difference in weight was enough to give me a skeletal appearance that made people think of what I might look like when I am old. Even my carefully-fitted tux hung on my bones.

Of course, Sallie's family knew of my recent illness. But I imagine they experienced a bit of dismay when they arrived for the wedding and got a fresh look at the gaunt man whom Sallie had agreed to marry.

It was March 20, 1976. Sallie and I were married at First Baptist Church of Wixom, Michigan, just northwest of Detroit. Her Uncle Jerry, a pastor for many years, performed the wedding ceremony. My parents could not afford to return from Africa for the wedding; my oldest brother, Phil, and his wife stood in for them in their absence.

We chose to be married in Wixom, because this was the center of the kingdom belonging to Sallie's family. Her parents now lived in New York, but this had been their home for many years. Sallie herself had lived her early childhood years in Wixom. Her grandparents, uncles and aunts and most of her cousins still lived in the area.

At our wedding, March 1976

Of course, we thought our wedding was beautiful – even if young people today laugh at some of our wedding pictures because of how the men were dressed. My white tux and white dress shoes bring a smile to our children, and they laugh out loud at the baby-blue tuxes worn by the best man and groomsmen!

In those days, it was not common for the engaged couple to tell people in advance what they wanted for wedding gifts, unless someone specifically asked for a suggestion. We certainly did not compile a wedding gift "registry" listing all the household items we would like people to buy for us.

It was enough for us to have a simple, tasteful reception offering cake and punch to our guests in the basement of the church. It was enough to know the love of our friends and family through gifts that they had chosen especially for us.

Knowing that we were headed for the wilds of Africa, one uncle gave us a gift which, when opened in front of the crowd, brought a laugh to everybody. It was an outdated Sears catalog, complete with a length of sturdy twine through the binding, by which this paper supply could be hung in the "outhouse." The label read, "For Those Who Lack the Finer Things in Life!"

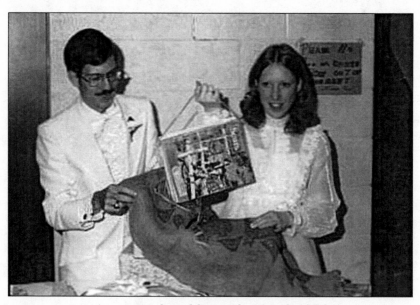

A practical wedding gift, March 1976

We finally left the church to begin our married life together – or I should say, we *tried* to leave the church. As we took our seats in our 1974 Chevrolet Nova, the uncles . . . or cousins . . . or brothers . . . or *whoever* . . . put rocks behind the rear wheels of the car so we couldn't back out of the parking space! I was obligated to get out of the car, find the problem and remove the rocks – all the while enduring the smirks on the faces of our watching "friends." As soon as I got back into the car, the rocks were quickly replaced. There was nothing to do but get out and remove the rocks again, and again, until finally the crowd tired of their sport and allowed us to leave.

This was late Saturday afternoon. We drove about an hour and stopped for supper on the outskirts of Toledo, Ohio. Back in the car, we drove through heavy rain for two and a half hours more, with Sallie doing everything she could to stop the incessant dripping from our leaky sunroof. We arrived late that evening in Cedarville, Ohio, where we spent our first night together in our own apartment.

We attended church the next morning in our own home church, Grace Baptist Church of Cedarville, before we headed south for what would be a four-month honeymoon!

I guess I should explain. We wanted some special time together in Florida. So I had arranged meetings, in Florida churches for the first month, then in other churches as we turned north toward Ohio, to preach and present our plans for overseas missionary work. One weekend during this extended honeymoon, for a church youth retreat in Florida, Sallie and I separated for a couple of nights to serve as counselors in the girls' and boys' cabins!

Oh, well, what did you *expect* of these young missionary appointees? Did you really expect we could spend four months in a plush Sheraton Hotel somewhere, lounging on the beach and sipping lemonade?

"You'll Never Be Able to Learn a Foreign Language"

Back in Cedarville, Ohio, as spring turned to summer, we settled into our ground-floor apartment and enjoyed the rest of our honeymoon – even as we pursued a full schedule of weekend meetings in Ohio and Pennsylvania.

Sallie used this break from her classes to complete her written application to become a BMM missionary, and to prepare for her doctrinal exam. In July Sallie faced the General Council as I had the previous November. As her husband, I could sit with her for moral support – and even give her a bit of help if she needed it – but she was expected to respond to all of the Council's questions herself.

Of course, Sallie was nervous like everyone who faced this examination. She did find some unexpected support, however, from the wife of a Council member who sat primly in the front row and smiled her encouragement at Sallie all the way through the ordeal. Sallie recalls how reassuring it was to her to realize that she had a friend in the room.

Several times during the questioning, one of the Council members sitting in the back interrupted, "Will you please speak up, young lady? We can't hear you here in the back."

Finally Sallie's friend in the front row spoke up, kindly but firmly rebuking the gentlemen in the back rows, "Why, from where I'm sitting I can hear her just fine. There are still seats up here in the front rows. If you really want to hear her, why don't you move up here?"

Larry and Sallie, summer 1976

Immediately following Sallie's successful doctrinal examination came two weeks of Candidate Seminar, required for all candidates before their official entrance into the Mission as appointees. That year, as they did for many years, BMM contracted to use the facilities of Cedarville College.

Even though we had an apartment in town, we were required to stay in the college dorm together with the thirty-plus candidates. That way we would have the full impact of the Candidate Seminar experience, and like the other candidates we could be observed in our interactions with each other and with the group.

Having attended Candidate Seminar before my short term in Africa, I was not required to attend all the seminar sessions with Sallie, but I chose to participate in most of their activities in order to be with her. Sallie had to take the required "Language Aptitude Test," but since I had taken it my first time around I did not take it again.

One of the expectations at the end of Candidate Seminar was a "candidate interview." Each candidate couple would meet with two or three mission administrators, including the one who would most likely be overseeing their long-term missionary work.

This was a time for straight talk, for counsel that would either confirm the candidates' future field and ministry or in some cases point them in a new, unexpected direction. Character flaws that had surfaced in the close dormitory life or under the pressure of the seminar schedule were sometimes addressed. Of course, our mission leaders were concerned for the long-term interests of both the Mission and the candidates themselves.

Sallie and I sat down together for our interview. "We know that you are focused on ministry in the Central African Republic," the administrators began. "You are aware that missionaries to CAR have to learn both *Sango*, the national language, and French, the 'official' language of the country."

"Yes, we're aware of this. We know it will be difficult – especially for Sallie, who has not had any background in either of those languages. But we will take it a little at a time, and we know God will help us."

Someone cleared his throat. "Well . . . , that's something about which we need to talk to you. In fact, Sallie, you failed the Language Aptitude Test . . . . And that tells us that you'll never be able to learn a foreign language. Not one – and certainly not *two*. Based on those results, we are obliged to tell you that we're not sure CAR is the best place for you. Maybe you should reconsider your choice of field."

Wow, that was quite a bombshell! We sat silent for a moment, digesting what we had heard. Then we quietly expressed our confidence that God had called us to CAR. "God will help us do what we must do, and over time Sallie will learn enough to get along."

Our first "prayer card," late summer 1976

Well, They Were Right . . . .

Let me jump forward in time and tell you how God helped us. We had been told that Sallie would never be able to learn a foreign language. "Not one – and certainly not *two*," our mission leaders had said. Well, they were right . . . . Sallie ended up learning not one language, and not two – *she ended up learning three foreign languages!*

Sallie managed quite well the nine months of French language study in Sherbrooke, Quebec (Canada). Through personal discipline and with God's help, by the end of that time she could get along okay in simple French.

When we transitioned almost immediately into *Sango* language study in Central African Republic, Sallie lost much of her fluency in French. You see, she was forced to shift her concentration from French to a different vocabulary and grammar. But *Sango* – a tonal language – was the language we would use every day in our ministry in CAR, so Sallie buckled down to learn the strange sounds. Slowly, over time, she became comfortable using this African language.

After three terms in CAR, we moved south to Zambia (Africa), to help Baptist Mid-Missions open a new work in that country. There we could get along in English, their "official" language. But we were determined to learn the predominant local language, *Nyanja*, in order to maximize our ability to communicate with the Zambians.

Sallie was one of eight American missionaries in our party who enrolled in *Nyanja* language lessons, taught by a German linguist who had settled in Zambia and made a living by teaching the *Nyanja* language to foreigners like ourselves.

At the end of the six-month course, all eight of us took the standardized *Nyanja* test – the same one taken by the American Embassy staff – to see how well we had done.

Who do you think got the best grade of the bunch of us? Not me, who had grown up surrounded by foreign languages and had studied linguistics in college. *Sallie got the best grade* – and this was her third foreign language. I was so proud of her! This was the same young lady who, by virtue of a Language Aptitude Test years earlier, had been judged incapable of learning even one foreign language.

Lest we be misunderstood, we know the value of godly counsel. We would never encourage anyone to take lightly the advice of those in authority over him. The leaders of our Mission have proven themselves worthy of our highest respect. God uses them to guide us!

But in this case we knew that God had called us to CAR, and we knew that He would help us do what we had to do. After all, we had the same confidence in God that Paul expressed in Philippians 4:13: "I can do all things through Christ who strengthens me."

A Perfect Father's Day Gift!

For four months Sallie had freed herself from the obligations of classes and work. Now she buckled down to finish her last year of classes. Her part-time nursing job, held for her until now, brought in some income to help with our expenses.

I continued to fulfill the church meetings that we had scheduled throughout the Midwest, even though I sometimes had to do those meetings by myself. You see, Sallie's responsibilities at school and work often made it impossible for her to travel with me.

Six months into our marriage, Sallie became pregnant with our first child. In spite of morning sickness, the pregnancy didn't interfere with her classes or work. Her college classes continued into the beginning of June, however, and Sallie found it more and more difficult to fit herself into the student desks. Her doctor said the baby could come any day. We weren't sure she would carry the baby long enough to finish her final exams.

Well, the baby did wait until Sallie completed her schooling. On Father's Day – Sunday, June 19, 1977 – Sallie delivered our first child, a daughter, Aimee Monique. What a perfect Father's Day gift for me! *You planned it that way for me, Sallie, didn't you?*

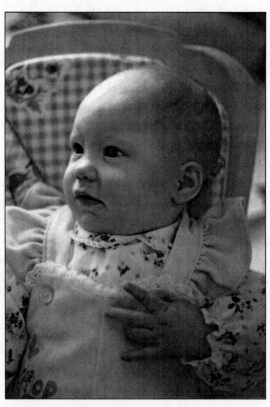

Our daughter Aimee, December 1977

Chickens and Dumpling (Sallie's Story)

Early in my pregnancy, while morning sickness was my constant companion, Larry made a weekend trip to Indiana without me. I had to work and also be ready for classes Monday morning.

That Sunday afternoon Larry accompanied the pastor on a visit to a farmer from the church. During the visit the farmer was lamenting a problem that had arisen on his farm. He thought he had successfully gotten rid of his flock of chickens only to be surprised by a hen that had been sitting on a hidden nest and now returned with a brood of half-grown chicks. They were growing quickly and the farmer really did want to be done with them. He was ready to give them away to accomplish the purpose.

Larry, being a good missionary, quickly said that in Africa he would never refuse an offer of a chicken. It was a common gift for the visiting speaker and offense would be taken if the gift was refused. To my surprise, Monday afternoon Larry returned home with seven chickens, legs bound, in the trunk of the car.

We lived in an apartment of a house that had been divided up with our apartment connecting to a small fenced backyard. Still, I did not think that it would be appropriate for us to have chickens in our backyard in the middle of the small town of Cedarville. Besides, the weather was getting colder and what would we feed them? And what would the neighbors think?

We had become friends with some of our neighbors, brothers from West Virginia who came to our aid. The plan was that Wayne and Paul would butcher the chickens if I would cook them. Larry helped where he could but the brothers definitely had the skills on this one.

After a flurry of backyard activity my dishpan returned to the kitchen, complete with dead, plucked, beheaded, gutted chickens. My stomach turned over and I bolted from the room. My grandparents had a chicken farm and I had experienced the process many times, but never combined with a pregnancy.

As I got things under control, the guys decided they were hungry and voted for chicken and dumplings. My refrigerator freezer was much too tiny to store the meat, so this was indeed the best solution.

However, it was getting late in the day and there was not time to boil the meat, cool it and pick all those tiny bones out before the guys died of starvation. Their decision was that we should just leave the bones in and pick them out as we ate. Remember, these were just half-grown chickens so even the drumsticks were not more than about three inches long.

Into my biggest pot went the chickens and seasonings and finally, on top, a double batch of dumplings, since these big guys were all so hungry!

My biggest pot was not nearly large enough. As the dumplings raised and cooked, they all congealed together into one large mass. Those guys from West Virginia sure teased me about my *chickens and dumpling*, but I will say it was tender and tasty, if you didn't mind picking out the bones (and there were lots of them)!

18

SO MUCH WAS NEW: 1976 – 1977

Everything Was Falling into Place

Our required financial support was in place by the summer of 1977. Raising our support had taken about eighteen months from the time I, Larry, was appointed in November 1975. This was less than the average of two years we had been told to expect. Of course, we had started with $300 per month support which continued after my short term in CAR.

Looking toward our ministry in CAR, we had purchased a brand-new 1976 model, "bahama blue," single cab, three-quarter-ton, four-wheel-drive, Ford F-250 Custom pickup, with a six-cylinder gasoline engine. We ordered it right from the factory, equipped the way we wanted it.

This new pickup lacked the luxury items – no radio or air-conditioning or cruise-control, for example. But it was heavy on the functional extras: the preferred manual transmission option, four-speed stick shift on the floor, woven-nylon seats for durability, dual gas tanks, dual heavy-duty batteries under the hood, oil-bath air cleaner, special lifetime fire-ignition spark plugs, electronic ignition to eliminate points and condenser (with spare electronic ignition module), exterior locking tool box built into the body, larger heavy-duty mud-lug tires . . . . What else am I forgetting?

Oh, it was quite a truck! Grateful for the help of our supporters, we paid a total of about $6,500 for it.

One of our supporting churches paid for the purchase of a new 1975 Yamaha 125cc street-and-trail motorcycle. We would load it into the back of the pickup for shipment to Africa when the time came for that. This full-size bike was street-legal, but equipped for the rugged trails on which I would use it in CAR.

We were so excited! Everything was falling into place.

It was our understanding that BMM missionaries heading to foreign-language fields in those years were expected to take a language-learning course at the Toronto Summer Institute of Linguistics. We should have done that in the summer of 1977, but somehow it did not happen. I don't even remember making a decision about it.

It seems that all our intentions regarding the language-learning course were swept away by our expectations of the baby's arrival early that summer and our departure later that summer for French language study.

Why French Too?

We would not be able to use English at all in Central African Republic, except in our own home and among the American missionaries.

The *Sango* language would be our means of everyday communication in CAR, and the language we would use for all our teaching and preaching.

French was the second language we would need to learn for our work in CAR. The French had colonized central Africa, and their language lingered on as the "official" language of the five independent nations which had until 1960 comprised the huge territory known as French Equatorial Africa.

If we would use *Sango* in our day-to-day lives and ministries, why would we need to know French too?

Many developing nations in the world, like these countries in the center of Africa, have their own languages but find themselves resorting to one major world language or another as their "official" language. This widely-known language is used in government, education and business and allows the otherwise isolated country to interact more easily with others in the world.

In fact anybody who is educated in CAR, for example, receives his middle and higher education in French. It is not his first language, but knowing French increases his potential for a better job and better income.

Any African without this French education is left behind in a rapidly advancing world. He will perhaps never move beyond the agrarian village life of his ancestors.

It can be said without risk of contradiction that, in CAR, knowing French definitely offers the missionary an added advantage. It gives the missionary an immediate way of communicating with the people until he learns *Sango*. It also helps him to learn *Sango,* since that language is built on the French phonetic system and incorporates some French words. In addition, it potentially opens the door to additional contacts and opportunities among the educated French speakers in the country.

France, Switzerland, or Canada?

It was time to take our next step toward the mission field.

Through the years, BMM missionaries had tried several options for French language study. The majority went to France for the training they needed, and some chose to go to Switzerland. A very few had tried Canada where, in a small Bible institute in Sherbrooke, Quebec, they found a French language training program geared especially for missionaries.

None of our BMM missionaries had tried Sherbrooke recently. But we liked what we discovered, as we compared this option with the others.

Everybody warned us that the variety of French spoken in Quebec is different from international French, and we knew that to be true. But we were given very strong assurance that the French training program in Sherbrooke was taught by French teachers *from France*, and that they were very intentional about guiding their missionary students to learn international French.

The cost of living and studying in Sherbrooke would be minimal, when compared with the anticipated costs in Europe.

And there was the added advantage of Sherbrooke being close to Ohio, just a twelve-hour drive away! Why was that important?

Because we could leave for language school when necessary that summer, without having to finalize our packing for CAR before leaving – as we would have to do if going to Europe to study. At the end of the school year in Canada, we would simply return to Ohio, finish our packing, then leave for Africa.

So the decision was made. With the agreement of BMM, we made plans to move to Canada for the nine months of the 1977-1978 school year.

BMM missionary Elaine Schulte, a nurse headed to Ivory Coast, was also from our hometown of Cedarville, Ohio. We were delighted that she decided to join us in Canada. This would allow us to continue what would become a lifelong friendship.

During the subsequent months in Canada we would also make friends with missionary students from several mission agencies. Our common purpose would unite us in a common bond, and the resulting camaraderie would help us face the overwhelming challenge called "language study."

Total Immersion

When we arrived in Sherbrooke, Canada, we rented an apartment and settled into the routine of French classes at Bethel Bible Institute. There were about twenty students in the Bible program and about the same number in the French language program. There was a comfortable family spirit on campus, and a lot of encouragement for us to succeed.

We were immersed in French, for everything here was taught in French and the Bible students' interaction with us was all in French.

We spent our mornings at Bethel, with one extended class each day to teach us French vocabulary and dialogue, and another to instruct us in French grammar. Plus we attended the daily chapel – where the singing, testimonies and messages were all in French.

Home in our apartment for the afternoon and evening, we spent the necessary hours to do our written homework and to sit with a tape recorder for the taped exercises. Some of these exercises demanded that we try to produce the correct translation from English to French, or from French to English – with immediate spoken confirmation of the correct answer. Other exercises required us to imitate as exactly as possible the pronunciation and flow of what the French speaker said. Over and over again we stumbled on the words, and then went back and did it again. We spent long hours on our homework every day.

As an MK in central Africa, I had heard French spoken around me, so I had that little bit of French background. Then I took three years of French in high school. So I was familiar with the language and could understand a little bit of what was going on around me. But I found that this intensive French study was a huge challenge for me!

And if *I* found it difficult, what must this immersion in French have been like for *Sallie*, whose only foreign language background was Spanish classes in high school! Oh, what a challenge she faced.

Aimee was just six weeks old when we made this transition to Canada. A nursery was provided for us during our morning class hours and that was a great help. In the afternoons, I tried to make things easier for Sallie by taking the responsibility for Aimee. That way Sallie could just concentrate on French.

So Sallie holed up in our bedroom with her books and papers and tape recorder, while I kept Aimee with me in the living room. I tried to occupy her while doing my homework. Fortunately, she was quite a happy and contented baby and did not cause me any great frustrations.

Aimee during our French language study, early 1978

Television in Sherbrooke gave us access to both French and English programming. Knowing the value of total immersion when learning a language, we allowed ourselves to listen only to French.

Of course we were not restricted to home and school. After trying several Baptist churches in the area we settled on a small independent Baptist church in Lennoxville, along with several of our classmates, and attended there every Sunday. More French exposure.

We were out in the community regularly for shopping, banking and other business. We tried to speak in French everywhere we went.

Some of the locals patiently put up with our halting French and even smiled their encouragement. Some, not so patient, grunted their frustration with our pitiful efforts before they themselves switched to English. Of course this effectively cut off the practice that would help us improve our French. Others accepted our best efforts, then answered in such rapid French that it was discouraging – as if they were trying to pass the message, "You might as well give up. You will never speak like we do."

It was painful, but there *was* progress. Sounds became intelligible words. Words became commonly used phrases, then full sentences. And those full sentences led to simple conversations.

Toward the end of the school year, each missionary in the French language program was scheduled to speak in chapel. He or she was to give his testimony and present his missionary ministry to the small student body – all in French, of course! As a couple, we made our well-rehearsed presentation together, with each of us contributing a fair portion of the speaking.

This event was challenging for each missionary – but somehow fun too, for now we found ourselves able to do something that we had not been able to do before. Each presentation was an occasion to celebrate our progress in French.

French . . . , French . . . , French. Nine months of total immersion. It was a test of our endurance. But endure we did. And *finally* it was over.

On Our Way to Africa

After our French language study was completed, we returned to Cedarville, Ohio. There was a flurry of shopping, packing, church meetings and final business details, as we prepared to leave for our missionary assignment in Central African Republic.

Our pickup truck, with its "cap" protecting the motorcycle and whatever other personal belongings we could fit inside, was sent on its way across land and sea. We would not see it again until, about five months later, it would arrive in port on the coast of Africa. With the help of an experienced missionary, I would personally collect the truck from the port authorities in Douala, Cameroon, and make the long drive inland to CAR.

Aimee, Sallie and Larry ready to head to NY with pickup and baggage to ship to Africa, July 1978

Time was short. Excitement about the future – and, yes, fears too – mixed with the pain of saying goodbye to our many friends and loved ones.

Then, all too suddenly, we were on our way to Africa.

In the last two and a half years we had faced so much that was new. Our new status with Baptist Mid-Missions as full-time missionaries, for example. Our new relationships to each other as husband

and wife, and then as parents to our baby girl. Our new friendships with churches who had chosen to partner with us in our ministry. Our newfound ability in French, however minimal.

Now we geared up for something else that was new.

I had grown up in Africa. Sallie had spent six weeks in Africa in BMM's apprenticeship program, so she knew a little bit about what was ahead. And I had done a fourteen-month stint in Africa as a short-term missionary.

But now we were going to Africa as a family. As career missionaries. We knew that this was a new phase in our lives. And we were very much aware that we needed God's help.

God, our confidence is in You. Please go with us.

Picture used for updated "prayer card," summer 1978, just before departure for Africa

CPSIA information can be obtained at www.ICGtesting.com
Printed in the USA
LVOW101436230911

247460LV00004BA/1/P